D1797841

RIBA Plan of Work 2013 Guide
Design Management

The RIBA Plan of Work 2013 Guides

Other titles in the series:

Project Leadership, by Nick Willars
Contract Administration, by Ian Davies
Town Planning, by Ruth Reed

Coming in 2015:

Information Exchanges
Sustainability
Conservation
Health and Safety
Handover Strategy

The RIBA Plan of Work 2013 is endorsed by the following organisations:

Royal Incorporation of
Architects in Scotland

Chartered Institute of
Architectural Technologists

Royal Society of
Architects in Wales

Construction
Industry Council

Royal Society
of Ulster Architects

RIBA Plan of Work 2013 Guide

Design
Management

Dale Sinclair

RIBA ⫙ **Publishing**

© RIBA Enterprises Ltd, 2014
Published by RIBA Publishing, The Old Post Office, St Nicholas Street,
Newcastle upon Tyne NE1 1RH

ISBN 978 1 85946 550 9
Stock code 82650

The right of Dale Sinclair to be identified as the Author of this Work has
been asserted in accordance with the Copyright, Designs and Patents
Act 1988 sections 77 and 78.

All rights reserved. No part of this publication may be reproduced,
stored in a retrieval system, or transmitted, in any form or by any
means, electronic, mechanical, photocopying, recording or otherwise,
without prior permission of the copyright owner.

British Library Cataloguing in Publication Data
A catalogue record for this book is available from the British Library.

Commissioning Editor: Sarah Busby
Series Editor: Dale Sinclair
Project Manager: Alasdair Deas
Design: Kneath Associates
Typesetting: Academic+Technical, Bristol, UK
Printed and bound by CPI Group (UK) Ltd
Cover image: © Simon Menges, Turner Contemporary

While every effort has been made to check the accuracy and quality
of the information given in this publication, neither the Author nor the
Publisher accept any responsibility for the subsequent use of this
information, for any errors or omissions that it may contain, or for any
misunderstandings arising from it.

RIBA Publishing is part of RIBA Enterprises Ltd
www.ribaenterprises.com

Contents

Foreword

This Design Management Guide is a timely publication, coming as it does at a point when the time pressures on the design process are so intense. In the pre-construction period, the design process is increasingly compacted into a shorter period as the wish to get on to site earlier with a high degree of cost certainty increases. There is then the conflicting requirement to manage design input that is prepared over an increasingly longer portion of the overall construction process – in particular, that undertaken by contactors and their specialist subcontractors generally simultaneously with the construction period. In such a pressured environment it is welcome to see a renewed focus on the role of the lead designer and the skills and tools needed in managing the production, coordination and integration of the design into the overall project.

In this context the comprehensive rethinking undertaken by the authors of the RIBA Plan of Work 2013 has brought a breadth and depth of clarity. Its focus on the flexibility needed to address different procurement routes, the emphasis on the collaborative nature of design and the integrated consideration of sustainability and digital design environments is resulting in a positive adoption across the industry. This guide, one of a suite supporting the RIBA Plan of Work 2013, now provides a valuable stage-by-stage route map to those undertaking the lead designer role.

In practice, of course, the design process rarely proceeds according to the strictly linear and ideal manner sometimes suggested by management guides; the reality is more often confused, exciting and dynamic, charged by conflicting commercial interests and coloured by the personalities involved.

Within this arena, the lead designer, armed with the guidance and the tools set out in this guide, and bolstered by their own strength of will and force of personality, will be better able to bring clarity of direction to and communication between the design team for the benefit of the project.

Whether for some, as the author says, design begins 'with a blank computer screen' or for others with an empty stretch of sketch roll and a pen, adequate time needs to be allowed at the earliest stages for the right design to develop if a robust strategy and clear direction are to be established for the project.

A strong lead designer has a key part to play in creating that time for design and, with the understanding that management is not an end in itself, but that designers are usually best placed to manage design, this renewed focus on the role can only be positive for the design professions.

Jonathan Hall
Director and Co-founder, Allford Hall Monaghan Morris

Series editor's foreword

The RIBA Plan of Work 2013 was developed in response to the needs of an industry adjusting to emerging digital design processes, disruptive technologies and new procurement models, as well as other drivers. A core challenge is to communicate the thinking behind the new RIBA Plan in greater detail. This process is made more complex because the RIBA Plan of Work has existed for 50 years and is embodied within the psyche and working practices of everyone involved in the built environment sector. Its simplicity has allowed it to be interpreted and used in many ways, underpinning the need to explain the content of the Plan's first significant edit. By relating the Plan to a number of commonly encountered topics, the *RIBA Plan of Work 2013 Guides* series forms a core element of the communication strategy and I am delighted to be acting as the series editor.

The first strategic shift in the RIBA Plan of Work 2013 was to acknowledge a change from the tasks of the design team to those of the project team: the client, design team and contractor. Stages 0 and 7 are part of this shift, acknowledging that buildings are used by clients, or their clients, and, more importantly, recognising the paradigm shift from designing for construction towards the use of high-quality design information to help facilitate better whole-life outcomes.

New procurement strategies focused around assembling the right project team are the beginnings of significant adjustments in the way that buildings will be briefed, designed, constructed, operated and used. Design teams are harnessing new digital design technologies (commonly bundled under the BIM wrapper), linking geometric information to new engineering analysis software to create a generation of buildings that would not previously have been possible. At the same time, coordination processes and environmental credentials are being improved. A core focus is the progressive fixity of high-quality information – for the first time, the right information at the right time, clearly defining who does what, when.

The RIBA Plan of Work 2013 aims to raise the knowledge bar on many subjects, including sustainability, Information Exchanges and health and safety. The *RIBA Plan of Work 2013 Guides* are crucial tools in disseminating and explaining how these themes are fully addressed and how the new Plan can be harnessed to achieve the new goals and objectives of our clients.

Dale Sinclair
November 2014

Acknowledgements and dedication

I would like to thank Adrian Dobson, RIBA Director of Practice, who was instrumental in kick-starting the development of the RIBA Plan of Work 2013, as well as the many architects who contributed to the development of the Plan. I would also like to thank the members of the various CIC groups who helped define the new project stages that are now integrated into the Plan.

This guide would not have been possible without the practical project experience I gained while working at BDP and Dyer and I would like to thank the directors of these companies and the many clients and design team collaborators who have provided their insights and contributions over the years.

My thanks also go to Sarah Busby from RIBA Publishing, who has patiently steered the series towards publication and facilitated the discussions required to ensure that the guides' themes are intrinsically linked to the RIBA Plan of Work 2013.

Finally, and most importantly, I would like to thank my wife, Stacy, for her patience and support and for constantly acting as a sounding board, and my daughter, Eilidh, for keeping her tiny fingers away from my keyboard.

About the author and series editor

Dale Sinclair is Director of Technical Practice for AECOM's architecture team in EMEA. He is an architect and was previously a director at Dyer and an associate director at BDP. He has taught at Aberdeen University and the Mackintosh School of Architecture and regularly lectures on BIM, design management and the RIBA Plan of Work 2013. He is passionate about developing new design processes that can harness digital technologies, manage the iterative design process and improve design outcomes.

He is currently the RIBA Vice President, Practice and Profession, a trustee of the RIBA Board, a UK board member of BuildingSMART and a member of various CIC working groups. He was the editor of the *BIM Overlay to the Outline Plan of Work 2007*, edited the RIBA Plan of Work 2013 and was author of its supporting tools and guidance publications: *Guide to Using the RIBA Plan of Work 2013* and *Assembling the Collaborative Project Team*.

Introduction

Overview

This guide considers the lead designer role, which is an important role on any project. Without the lead designer's input the architect's Concept Design can be diluted as it progresses beyond Stage 2. Design quality is greatly impacted by the quality of the coordination work undertaken by the lead designer at Stage 3. Stage 4 is no different. During that stage the lead designer must integrate any specialist subcontractor design work into the coordinated design while also marshalling and reviewing any further information produced by the design team for construction. The lead designer needs to make sure that the contractor receives the right information at the right time, bearing in mind that, on most projects, Stages 4 and 5 will overlap.

The lead designer's role is becoming more complex. Design information that was hitherto produced solely for construction purposes is increasingly being used for a greater number of operational and/or asset management purposes. The RIBA Plan of Work 2013 contains two new stages – Stage 7 (In Use) and Stage 0 (Strategic Definition) – which underpin this new requirement. The lead designer may not always be involved in these new stages, but they will lead the stages when these new information requirements are being produced. The lead designer therefore has a vested interest in understanding these important new stages. While the majority of this publication focuses on the core design stages (Stages 2, 3 and 4), where the lead designer role is crucial, it also considers how the lead designer's skills and insight might add value to these new project stages and how, in turn, this will lead to better Project Outcomes for clients.

Context

There are three core design stages: Stage 2: Concept Design, Stage 3: Developed Design and Stage 4: Technical Design. Stage 2 commences with a 'blank screen' and Stage 4 concludes with a substantial amount of information. Navigating through these stages can be challenging, regardless of the client, the brief, the complexity of the project, the sector or the challenges presented by a specific site. The lead designer's role is crucial if the diversity of these design stages is to be successfully managed and the design management skills, tools and experience required at each stage will vary from project to project.

The core project leadership roles that work alongside the RIBA Plan of Work 2013 have been amended and adjusted to bring greater clarity to the leadership roles within the project team. The core leadership roles are:

the client, who is responsible for the strategic direction of the project and key project decisions

the project lead, who is responsible for assembling and managing the project team, which comprises the client, the design team and the contractor

the lead designer, who is responsible for leading and managing the design work of the design team, and

the contractor, who is responsible for the construction and the design work of various specialist subcontractors (and the design team, depending on the procurement route).

The diagram in figure 1 considers the core entities that form the project team. This structure avoids ambiguity in relation to the design process: the lead designer is responsible for leading the design process and the design team and for carrying out the design management tasks associated with this, including the preparation of a Design Programme at each stage.

Figure 1   The project team

Another core challenge for the lead designer is to consider how different procurement routes impact on the design process. This is considered in Stages 2 to 4. The diagram in figure 1 assists thinking in this regard: different forms of procurement assemble the client, the design team and the contractor in different ways. A core consideration arising from the RIBA Plan of Work 2013 is the extent of involvement the lead designer has in the selection of the design team that they will be responsible for managing. Where possible, the lead designer should be central to assembling the design team and, increasingly, employing the design team members, regardless of the form of procurement. On smaller or less complex projects it is acknowledged that the architect will also be acting as the project lead, lead designer and contract administrator. This publication considers the lead designer role independently, but the tips and tools are equally applicable to projects of any size and scale and regardless of the other roles which the lead designer may be undertaking.

How to use this book

This guide does not dwell on the contractual relationships between design team members as this is covered in greater in detail in

Assembling a Collaborative Project Team, nor does it consider what makes a collaborative team. With the lead designer now focused on the management of the design team, this guide is principally concerned with the subject of design management and how the lead designer can more effectively lead the work of the design team. More specifically, the book focuses on the task bars of the RIBA Plan of Work 2013 and the activities driven by each task bar. While it provides a detailed insight into the tasks contained within the RIBA Plan of Work 2013, it considers each of those tasks primarily from the lead designer's perspective.

Dale Sinclair
November 2014

Using this series

For ease of reference each book in this series is broken down into chapters that map on to the stages of the Plan of Work. So, for instance, the first chapter covers the tasks and considerations around design management at Stage 0.

We have also included several in-text features to enhance your understanding of the topic. The following key will explain what each icon means and why each feature is useful to you:

 The 'Example' feature explores an example from practice, either real or theoretical

 The 'Tools and Templates' feature outlines standard tools, letters and forms and how to use them in practice

 The 'Signpost' feature introduces you to further sources of trusted information from books, websites and regulations

 The 'Definition' feature explains key terms in this topic area in more detail

 The 'Hints and Tips' feature dispenses pragmatic advice and highlights common problems and solutions

 The 'Small Project Observation' feature highlights useful variations in approach and outcome for smaller projects

RIBA

The **RIBA Plan of Work 2013** organises the process of briefing, designing, constructing, maintaining, operating and using building projects into a number of key stages. The content of stages may vary or overlap to suit specific project requirements.

RIBA Plan of Work 2013

Stages

Tasks	0 Strategic Definition	1 Preparation and Brief	2 Concept Design	3 Developed Design
Core Objectives	Identify client's **Business Case** and **Strategic Brief** and other core project requirements.	Develop **Project Objectives**, including **Quality Objectives** and **Project Outcomes**, **Sustainability Aspirations**, **Project Budget**, other parameters or constraints and develop **Initial Project Brief**. Undertake **Feasibility Studies** and review of **Site Information**.	Prepare **Concept Design**, including outline proposals for structural design, building services systems, outline specifications and preliminary **Cost Information** along with relevant **Project Strategies** in accordance with **Design Programme**. Agree alterations to brief and issue **Final Project Brief**.	Prepare **Developed Design**, including coordinated and updated proposals for structural design, building services systems, outline specifications, **Cost Information** and **Project Strategies** in accordance with **Design Programme**.
Procurement *Variable task bar	Initial considerations for assembling the project team.	Prepare **Project Roles Table** and **Contractual Tree** and continue assembling the project team.	⇐ The procurement strategy does not fundamentally alter the progression of the design or the level of detail prepared at	a given stage. However, **Information Exchanges** will vary depending on the selected procurement route and **Building Contract**. A bespoke **RIBA Plan of Work**
Programme *Variable task bar	Establish **Project Programme**.	Review **Project Programme**.	Review **Project Programme**.	⇐ The procurement route may dictate the **Project Programme** and result in certain stages overlapping
(Town) Planning *Variable task bar	Pre-application discussions.	Pre-application discussions.	⇐ Planning applications are typically made using the Stage 3 output.	A bespoke **RIBA Plan of Work 2013** will identify when the
Suggested Key Support Tasks	Review **Feedback** from previous projects.	Prepare **Handover Strategy** and **Risk Assessments**. Agree **Schedule of Services**, **Design Responsibility Matrix** and **Information Exchanges** and prepare **Project Execution Plan** including **Technology** and **Communication Strategies** and consideration of **Common Standards** to be used.	Prepare **Sustainability Strategy, Maintenance and Operational Strategy** and review **Handover Strategy** and **Risk Assessments**. Undertake third party consultations as required and any **Research and Development** aspects. Review and update **Project Execution Plan**. Consider **Construction Strategy**, including offsite fabrication, and develop **Health and Safety Strategy**.	Review and update **Sustainability, Maintenance and Operational** and **Handover Strategies** and **Risk Assessments**. Undertake third party consultations as required and conclude **Research and Development** aspects. Review and update **Project Execution Plan, including Change Control Procedures**. Review and update **Construction** and **Health and Safety Strategies**.
Sustainability Checkpoints	**Sustainability Checkpoint — 0**	**Sustainability Checkpoint — 1**	**Sustainability Checkpoint — 2**	**Sustainability Checkpoint — 3**
Information Exchanges (at stage completion)	**Strategic Brief**.	**Initial Project Brief**.	**Concept Design** including outline structural and building services design, associated **Project Strategies**, preliminary **Cost Information** and **Final Project Brief**.	**Developed Design**, including the coordinated architectural, structural and building services design and updated **Cost Information**.
UK Government Information Exchanges	Not required.	Required.	Required.	Required.

*Variable task bar – in creating a bespoke project or practice specific RIBA Plan of Work 2013 via www.ribaplanofwork.com a specific bar is selected from a number of options.

The **RIBA Plan of Work 2013** should be used solely as guidance for the preparation of detailed professional services contracts and building contracts.

www.ribaplanofwork.com

4 Technical Design	5 Construction	6 Handover and Close Out	7 In Use
Prepare **Technical Design** in accordance with **Design Responsibility Matrix** and **Project Strategies** to include all architectural, structural and building services information, specialist subcontractor design and specifications, in accordance with **Design Programme**.	Offsite manufacturing and onsite **Construction** in accordance with **Construction Programme** and resolution of **Design Queries** from site as they arise.	Handover of building and conclusion of **Building Contract**.	Undertake **In Use** services in accordance with **Schedule of Services**.
2013 will set out the specific tendering and procurement activities that will occur at each stage in relation to the chosen procurement route.	Administration of **Building Contract**, including regular site inspections and review of progress.	Conclude administration of **Building Contract**.	
or being undertaken concurrently. A bespoke **RIBA Plan of Work 2013** will clarify the stage overlaps.	The **Project Programme** will set out the specific stage dates and detailed programme durations.		
planning application is to be made.			
Review and update **Sustainability, Maintenance and Operational** and **Handover Strategies** and **Risk Assessments**. Prepare and submit Building Regulations submission and any other third party submissions requiring consent. Review and update **Project Execution Plan**. Review **Construction Strategy**, including sequencing, and update **Health and Safety Strategy**.	Review and update **Sustainability Strategy** and implement **Handover Strategy**, including agreement of information required for commissioning, training, handover, asset management, future monitoring and maintenance and ongoing compilation of '**As-constructed' Information**. Update **Construction** and **Health and Safety Strategies**.	Carry out activities listed in **Handover Strategy** including **Feedback** for use during the future life of the building or on future projects. Updating of **Project Information** as required.	Conclude activities listed in **Handover Strategy** including **Post-occupancy Evaluation**, review of **Project Performance, Project Outcomes** and **Research and Development** aspects. Updating of **Project Information**, as required, in response to ongoing client **Feedback** until the end of the building's life.
Sustainability Checkpoint — 4	Sustainability Checkpoint — 5	Sustainability Checkpoint — 6	Sustainability Checkpoint — 7
Completed **Technical Design** of the project.	'**As-constructed' Information**.	Updated '**As-constructed' Information**.	'**As-constructed' Information** updated in response to ongoing client **Feedback** and maintenance or operational developments.
Not required.	Not required.	Required.	As required.

© RIBA

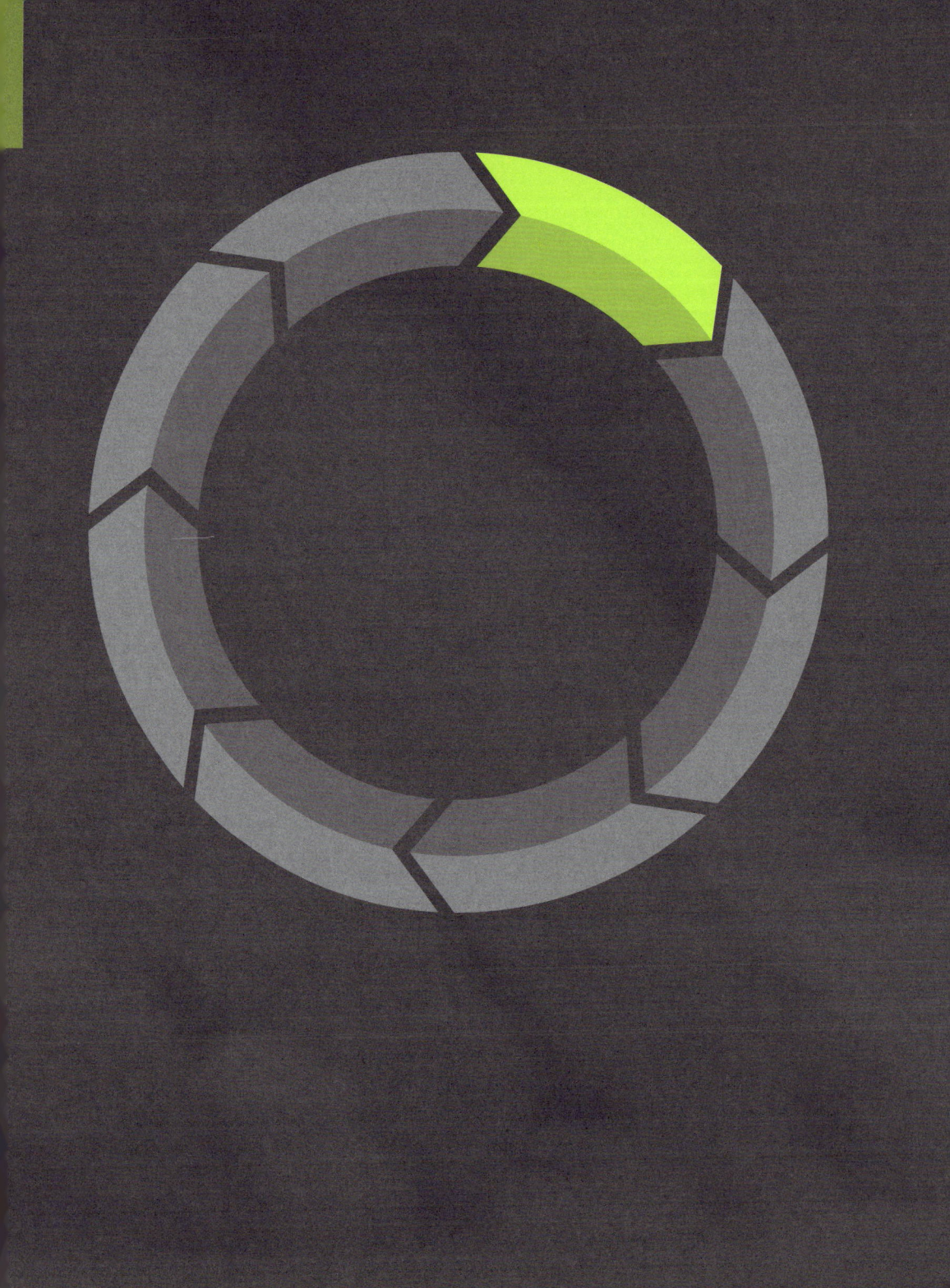

Stage 0

Strategic Definition

Chapter overview

Stage 0 is a new stage within the RIBA Plan of Work 2013. Its purpose is simple: to ensure that a building project is the best way of achieving the client's desired Project Outcomes. When the Business Case is considered by the project team at Stage 0 it should determine the most appropriate way forward before the Strategic Brief is defined and concluded. In the future, as increasingly more data become available, clients will be able to use Feedback from previous projects more objectively to inform both their Business Case and the contents of the Strategic Brief. The lead designer is unlikely to be directly involved at Stage 0 as there is no design to be managed. However, it is crucial that anyone undertaking the lead designer role understands the tasks and Information Exchanges undertaken during this stage as they strategically frame the design stages that will take place later.

The key coverage in this chapter is as follows:

What are the Core Objectives of Stage 0?

What procurement activities are required at Stage 0?

Why is the Project Programme crucial at Stage 0?

Why are town planning considerations important at Stage 0?

What supporting tasks should be undertaken during Stage 0?

Why are Sustainability Checkpoints important at this early stage?

What Information Exchanges occur at Stage 0?

What are the aims of the Government Information Exchanges task bar?

Introduction

Stage 0 is a crucial project stage. It allows a thorough examination of the client's Business Case and other core project requirements in order to generate the Strategic Brief that will, in turn, act as the basis for the more detailed Initial Project Brief produced at Stage 1.

Even on a smaller project considering the Business Case is essential. For example, if a family are considering a house extension, what is the rationale behind it? Do they like the area, the schools and wish more space? Will their initial thoughts increase the value of their property? Can other solutions deliver what they are looking for? Is it a short-term solution or are they planning to stay in the house over a long period? Put another way, the Strategic Definition stage considers the fundamental aspects of the project and encourages consideration of strategic aspects rather than immediately delving into the detail when the strategy may be wrong in the first place.

The project team formed at Stage 0 is likely to consist of a number of core advisers. These advisers may depend on who has established contact with the client, on the sector and/or the size and complexity of a project. The timescales involved will vary. On smaller projects a few days, or even hours, may be all that is required to conclude this stage whereas on larger or more complex projects a number of months may be required to analyse various data, commission studies that might influence the decision-making process and properly consider the client's requirements.

While the lead designer's skills are not essential at Stage 0, in some instances they may be indirectly involved. For example, on a smaller project the architect is likely to be carrying out the project lead, lead designer and other project roles and therefore undertaking the Stage 0 and 1 tasks. They can therefore be mindful during these stages of the developments from the lead designer's perspective. This chapter considers the activities undertaken during this stage and how they might influence the role and tasks of the lead designer in future stages.

What are the Core Objectives of this stage?

The Core Objectives of the RIBA Plan of Work 2013 at Stage 0 are:

Tasks ▼	**0** Strategic Definition
Core Objectives	Identify client's **Business Case** and **Strategic Brief** and other core project requirements.

The tasks at Stage 0 are strategic in nature. They consist of identifying the client's Business Case and, following its interrogation and adjustment (if required), preparing a Strategic Brief. Put another way, Stage 0 is not about creating a detailed brief – it is about ensuring that a robust strategic decision-making process has been adhered to, thereby avoiding abortive work in the later stages, when the amount of work undertaken by all members of the project team, and the associated costs, ramp up significantly.

What is a Business Case?

Put simply, the Business Case is the reasoning for undertaking a project. It might consist solely of a written statement, or it could contain references to the financial calculations or models that support and underpin the decision-making process. At the end of Stage 0 the Strategic Brief could actually conclude that a building project is not the right approach to deliver the desired Project Outcomes set out in the Business Case.

Of course, before the Business Case can be made the client must decide which advisers to appoint. This is a core task because different project teams at Stage 0 might deliver different results. Appointing the right project team with the right skills is therefore a crucial client activity.

Where different scenarios might achieve the same Project Outcomes, a means of comparing and scoring them objectively in order to decide the way forward may be required. In some instances, it may be appropriate to undertake some Stage 1 activities at Stage 0. For example, if a number of sites are being considered it would be wise to appraise each site and consider their pros and cons and how the building as envisaged might fit onto them (or not, as the case may be). This underlines a crucial aspect of the RIBA Plan of Work 2013: it is a guidance document. It cannot possibly set out all the tasks or Information Exchanges that could be appropriate at each stage of a project. These can vary significantly depending on the scale of the project, the sector involved and any unique aspects of the project. Those using the new plan should be mindful of this, and that it should be used as a flexible tool and not seen as a straightjacket.

The Business Case might contain:

I the appraisals from a number of sites
I the drivers behind the proposed project and the outcomes that are being sought
I a high-level cost study
I examples of suitable precedents, to allow quality aspirations to be understood.

The contents will vary from project to project; however, it is crucial that any drivers or influencing factors are recorded and signed off by the client.

What topics should the Strategic Brief address?

The Strategic Brief should summarise the conclusions from the Business Case in sufficient detail to give the party preparing the Initial Project Brief at Stage 1 a flying start and, more crucially, an understanding of the strategic boundaries of the project.

The Strategic Brief might set out:

| the strategic Project Outcomes derived from the Business Case
| the Project Budget
| core operational adjacencies and requirements
| high-level Sustainability Aspirations
| high-level area requirements and benchmarked net:gross area ratio.

Strategic Brief

The Strategic Brief is considered further in the *RIBA Plan of Work 2013 Guide: Project Leadership*.

What other core project requirements would be considered?

The 'other core project requirements' would comprise any aspects of the project that impact on the Strategic Brief. As noted above, Project Outcomes, site appraisals or other elements noted in the Stage 1 Core Objectives may impact on strategic considerations and so may need earlier consideration. A careful and judicious view needs to be taken to ensure that the right aspects are considered, and that not too much detail is developed. For example, it is unlikely that any of the Suggested Key Support Tasks from Stage 1, such as preparing the Project Execution Plan or considering the Design Responsibility Matrix, would add value to the preparation of the Strategic Brief.

What procurement activities are required at Stage 0?

The RIBA Plan of Work 2013 encourages initial consideration on assembling the project team at Stage 0. A major conundrum is how the Stage 0 team is kick-started. It is inevitable that the party who gets their foot in the door will be influential in determining how the project team is assembled. It is important for a client to ensure that whoever is appointed for Stage 0 has the skills and experience relevant to the stage. On smaller projects the architect may be the first point of contact. In these situations, where it is likely that the architect will also act as the lead designer, the lead designer's interests will, by default, be carefully considered.

Another Stage 0 consideration is that the Stage 1 project team will need to be appointed in sufficient time to commence their duties. If contractor-led procurement is being considered, the Stage 1 project team will need particular skills because the Initial Project Brief will act as the Employer's Requirements, the core tender document, and the content and format of the Information Exchange will need to be more structured and robust. This is considered further in the next stage (see page 31).

On other forms of procurement the project lead will need to appoint a design team prior to Stage 2 commencing. *Assembling a Collaborative Project Team* and the following chapters consider the tasks that have to be carried out to address this important activity.

Why is the Project Programme crucial at Stage 0?

The overall timescale for the Project Programme is a core strategic consideration. A major conundrum at Stage 0 is that the client may not have any specific constraints or timescales, in which case indicative programme timescales can be discussed. A more considered and detailed Project Programme can then be delivered at Stage 1, when it is likely that more project team members have been appointed and the brief and other project matters have been considered in greater detail.

Where the client's timescales are driven by a specific date, such as the beginning of a university year or the opening ceremony of a major sports event, the Project Programme will be an essential document at Stage 0, to demonstrate that the client's Project Programme aspirations are achievable. Where the Project Programme is not realistic, it is essential that the project team advise the client accordingly. In instances where a programme might be achievable by compressing timescales and/or overlapping activities and stages, the risks of doing so should be flagged to the client and recorded in the Strategic Brief. In such instances it is essential that a 'float', or contingency, exists in the Project Programme to deal with the many issues that may result in a delay.

The contents of the Project Programme are considered in greater detail in the next chapter (see page 37–9).

Why are town planning considerations important at Stage 0?

The importance of town planning considerations at Stage 0 will depend on the specifics of a project and the location of the site. For example, if the building requires a change of use or contradicts the local plan then clearly planning will be a strategic issue that needs to be addressed as part of Stage 0. Early consultations with the planners will be essential in developing a strategy, and in certain instances specific guidance from a planning consultant may also be required to inform the client's decision making. Conversely, if an extension to a house is proposed and it fits within local guidelines for permitted development and there are similar completed adjacent extensions then the converse will be true. Ultimately, a judgement call needs to be made, although a quick discussion with a planning officer may help reveal any particular issues that should be addressed in the Initial Project Brief at Stage 1.

Town planning

More detailed considerations for Stage 0 in relation to town planning are set out in the *RIBA Plan of Work 2013 Guide: Town Planning*.

What supporting tasks should be undertaken during Stage 0?

There is only one Suggested Key Support Task at Stage 0:

I Review Feedback from previous projects.

This task underlines the value that completing a Stage 7 to Stage 0 loop can bring at a strategic level. Data from previous projects can be crucial in informing the briefing process, starting with the compilation of the Strategic Brief, as well as the development of the Business Case.

Feedback is playing an increasingly crucial role on projects. An ever increasing amount of data is becoming available for mining and interpreting and it will increasingly become possible to use this data to inform the Strategic Brief. Smart sensor technologies will broaden the amount of data that can be obtained from Stage 7: In Use, allowing such data to inform future projects. Feedback harnessed at Stage 0 might comprise:

I data from footfall counters, used to assess circulation patterns from previous retail projects
I data from carbon dioxide sensors, used to measure room utilisation on education projects
I patient data, analysed to determine if recovery times have been improved in a hospital.

The inclusion of Feedback within the RIBA Plan of Work 2013 is an important addition as it encourages the use of In Use information from other projects by the same client, design or project team and completes the Stage 7 to Stage 0 loop. Open data initiatives will make much of this currently closed data.

Feedback on other elements, such as Project Outcomes, Quality Objectives including design quality and cost benchmarking, will also become more commonplace, allowing greater consideration of how previous projects have performed when considering the strategic aspects of a new project.

Why are Sustainability Checkpoints important at this early stage?

The RIBA Plan of Work 2013 does not specifically mention the client's Sustainability Aspirations until Stage 1; however, it may be necessary to consider any strategic points at Stage 0, particularly if a client places Sustainability Aspirations high on their list of subjects that a project must successfully address. It may be necessary to consider sustainability drivers as part of the Business Case, particularly if they impact on costs. If a number of sites are being considered, sustainability may be a significant driver in the appraisal and selection of a site. For example, refurbishing a city centre building will be a more sustainable approach than building on a greenfield site.

The online version of the RIBA Plan of Work 2013 set out the Sustainability Checkpoints. These detail some of the items that clients might consider as they develop their Strategic Brief.

What Information Exchanges occur at Stage 0?

The Information Exchange at Stage 0 is straightforward: the Strategic Brief.

What are the aims of the UK Government Information Exchanges task bar?

The RIBA Plan of Work 2013 sets out at each stage whether or not the government requires an Information Exchange. Information Exchanges are not required at certain stages because they are deemed to be contractual requirements between the design team and the contractor or between the contractor and any specialist subcontractors, and as such require no intervention from the government client. From the lead designer's perspective, the issues relevant to this topic are covered in the Information Exchanges task bar text and as such the UK Government Information Exchanges task bar is not considered further in this publication.

Chapter summary | 0

Stage 0 considers the strategic aspects of a project in order to ratify that a building project will deliver the desired Project Outcomes. This is particularly important in the context of sustainability and it is, of course, possible that the Strategic Brief may conclude that a space-planning exercise, refurbishment or extension to an existing building may be more appropriate than a new-build project. The goal of Stage 0 is to ensure that the high-level considerations and decision-making processes are robust. The activity required to support the Business Case will vary from project to project and should be carefully considered if the aim of Stage 0 is to be achieved, remembering that a robust Strategic Brief will prevent abortive work in the later project stages.

Preparation and Brief

Chapter overview

This chapter explains why Stage 1 is such a crucial project stage, particularly in relation to the work of the lead designer at Stage 2, when the design process begins in earnest. It considers the importance of the Initial Project Brief from the lead designer's perspective and what subjects require particular attention in terms of design management. During Stage 1 the project lead will assemble the project team. This will require preparation of core documents such as the Design Responsibility Matrix. The lead designer must check such documents rigorously as they fundamentally frame what is required at Stage 2 and, more importantly, establish what the other design team members have been appointed to do.

The key coverage in this chapter is as follows:

What are the Core Objectives of Stage 1?

What procurement activities are necessary at Stage 1?

Why is the Project Programme crucial at Stage 1?

How might town planning influence Stage 1?

What supporting tasks should be undertaken during Stage 1?

Why are Sustainability Checkpoints important?

What are the Stage 1 Information Exchanges?

Introduction

With Stage 0 having set the strategic framework for a project in the Strategic Brief and Project Programme, Stage 1 can begin in earnest, layering detail onto these documents. Stage 1 of the RIBA Plan of Work 2013 is a crucial project stage. Some might question this as no design or construction-related activity takes place, but the premise behind this stage is simple: if the Initial Project Brief is robust and comprehensively considered, and the project team has been assembled in a manner where each party knows what they have to do, when they have to do it and how they will do it, then Stage 2, and the subsequent stages, will be more efficient and effective.

This chapter considers why Stage 1 is of particular importance to the lead designer and the items that might be considered in relation to this subject. *Assembling a Collaborative Project Team* advocates the appointment of the design team by the end of Stage 1, ready for commencement of Stage 2. A major conundrum from the lead designer's perspective is that many of the core documents used while they are undertaking their design management duties, such as the Project Execution Plan, Design Responsibility Matrix and Information Exchanges, may have been generated, determined or influenced by others prior to their own involvement.

Certainly, where one party (likely to be the project lead at Stage 1) has developed the Design Responsibility Matrix and other core design-related documents for the design team, the lead designer should stringently check these documents prior to concluding their own professional services contract. This review would consider and include all of the design team members' professional services contracts, allowing the lead designer to be satisfied that each design team member is appointed in a manner that will deliver the right information at the right time.

A review should be undertaken regardless of who will appoint the design team members (the client, the contractor or the lead designer) because each design team member's Information Exchanges impact on the lead designer's ability to carry out their duties to coordinate at Stage 3 and integrate at Stage 4. The lead designer is increasingly responsible for appointing the design team. In these situations they will be responsible for all design aspects and their professional services contract will not need to contain the same granularity in relation to design responsibility. The lead designer will, however, need to ensure that each design team member's professional services contract (possibly a subcontract) specifies the individual degree of design responsibility precisely. Such documents may be derived from templates or may have been generated by the lead designer and fine-tuned over a number of projects.

There are currently initiatives encouraging standard industry deliverables documents. Such initiatives are welcome and would make the preparation by the project lead and the checking by the lead designer more straightforward and the transition to Stage 2 easier.

What are the Core Objectives of this stage?

The Core Objectives of the RIBA Plan of Work 2013 at Stage 1 are:

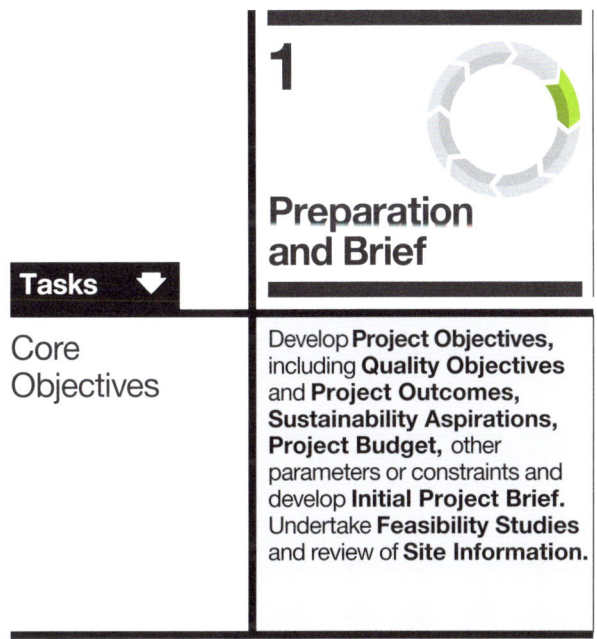

Tasks ▼	**1** Preparation and Brief
Core Objectives	Develop **Project Objectives,** including **Quality Objectives** and **Project Outcomes, Sustainability Aspirations, Project Budget,** other parameters or constraints and develop **Initial Project Brief.** Undertake **Feasibility Studies** and review of **Site Information.**

The Core Objectives at Stage 1 revolve around the preparation of the Initial Project Brief. As set out in the RIBA Plan of Work 2013, in order to prepare the brief the Project Objectives, including the Quality Objectives and Project Outcomes, Sustainability Aspirations, Project Budget and other parameters or constraints must be developed in order to put more flesh onto the bones of the Strategic Brief produced during Stage 0. The specific purpose of each of these defined terms, from the lead designer's perspective, is considered below.

Although a site may have been appraised and selected at Stage 0, Feasibility Studies may also be required during Stage 1 to test certain aspects of the developing brief against the chosen site. Good quality Site Information will assist the preparation of any such studies, but more importantly this information will be a core requirement for Stage 2, along with a robust Project Budget. These points are considered further below.

What are the Project Objectives?

Once the Strategic Brief has been signed off by the client, Stage 1 and the preparation of the Initial Project Brief can begin in earnest. The Strategic Brief should contain sufficient information on the Project Objectives. During Stage 1 the brief is further developed to consider the detail that will support these objectives. Two core aspects to be considered are the Quality Objectives and the Project Outcomes:

| Quality Objectives

Quality Objectives relate primarily to design quality and can cover a diverse range of subjects, such as finishes, products, or the quality of core spaces. When setting Quality Objectives, it is extremely helpful to visit exemplar projects with the client. This allows likes and dislikes to be determined, minimising the risk of the design team taking an approach that will not be supported by the client. In some instances an architect will be chosen because the client has seen and liked previous projects that they have undertaken. In these situations it may be less necessary to set Quality Objectives.

| Project Outcomes

Project Outcomes are a crucial new inclusion in the RIBA Plan of Work 2013. While the Quality Objectives might focus on the building as an output, the Project Outcomes will consider the business or other In Use outcomes that the client may wish to achieve. Examples might include:
o reduced reoffending rates for a new prison
o improved examination results for a new school
o shorter recovery times for a new hospital.

On receiving the Initial Project Brief the lead designer should not focus on how the client's desired Project Outcomes will be achieved, but on how the design team might be able to address and respond to each stated outcome at each stage. In the future, certain Project Outcomes will become more contractual in their nature; for example, the Building Contract could set a cap on the energy use of a building. How to measure the design at each project stage against the set Project Outcomes is a core consideration for the lead designer, as well as for the project lead, who may need to carry out the measurement.

Why are the Sustainability Aspirations a crucial consideration within the brief?

For a robust Concept Design to be delivered at the end of Stage 2 the design process must be undertaken in a holistic manner. As the Sustainability Aspirations of different clients may vary it is essential that these are considered at Stage 1 and integrated successfully into the Initial Project Brief. The Sustainability Aspirations would cover items such as:

I assessments to be undertaken and rating achieved (eg BREEAM Outstanding)
I energy targets including embodied energy and carbon
I the extent of community involvement and consultation.

Sustainability can heavily influence the design process, and so upon receipt of the Initial Project Brief the lead designer needs to consider how the design team might respond to the Sustainability Aspirations. Are they clear and unambiguous? Are they sufficiently well framed to be interpreted correctly by the design team? The aspirations also need to be reviewed against other Stage 1 information. For example, are there any contradictory statements in the Initial Project Brief and is the Project Budget sufficient to deliver the specific project Sustainability Aspirations?

What is the Project Budget and how might it influence the brief?

The Project Budget sets out the funds that the client has availability to complete a project. It might include budgets for:

I professional fees
I surveys
I construction work
I items directly supplied by the client (such as furniture or maintenance equipment)
I fees for statutory submissions
I furniture, fixtures and equipment (FF&E) works
I VAT.

While it is likely that the party undertaking the cost consultant role will prepare the Project Budget, both the project lead and the lead designer have a vested interest in ensuring that the budget is robust, remembering that on smaller projects the same practice may be carrying out both roles.

The lead designer may wish to ensure that the Project Budget includes sufficient fee allowances for all members of the design team, who will be appointed for the duration of the project. However, a core concern is ensuring that the budget for the construction work is realistic and will deliver the desired Project Objectives. In this regard, the lead designer should be mindful that, simplistically, the construction budget = the gross area in sq metres × the build cost per sq metre:

| Area

In many instances the Initial Project Brief will contain an area schedule developed with the client. If the schedule is not robust, the Concept Design could exceed the allocated area, requiring a larger Project Budget. It needs to be remembered that the construction budget is based on gross areas, whereas briefing schedules typically consider the precise and specific net areas required by the client. The allocation of allowances for circulation, staircases, toilets, plant spaces etc is therefore a crucial consideration at Stage 1: if these areas are exceeded in the Concept Design it is inevitable that the design will be over budget. The lead designer's main interest in relation to the brief (typically prepared by the project lead, perhaps with the assistance of a client adviser) is therefore arguably not defining the spaces that are required, but ensuring that allowances for the spaces that are not defined are proper and appropriate, ideally by benchmarking against other similar projects.

| Build cost per sq metre

If the sector norm for a building is a cost of £X per sq metre, but the client wants a project with a quality above the norm, for example a high-quality headquarters building or residential project, then it logically follows that a budget greater than £X per sq metre will be required. As the cost consultant is likely to set the initial area rate, the lead designer should be satisfied that, in their experience, it will deliver the desired Quality Objectives or other aspirations of the client.

The lead designer may not have contributed to the development of the Project Budget or have the knowledge to comment on it; however, it is essential that the lead designer's experience is used to ensure that all elements that have contributed to the development of the Project Budget have been properly considered and are aligned with the client's Project Objectives. Put another way, the lead designer should ensure that the

Example of area and per sq metre rate defining the estimated construction cost

Gross area		Cost/m²		Construction cost estimate
12,500 m²	×	**£1,400**	=	**£17.5m**
The anticipated area of functional brief is 10,000 m². The area of circulation and other non-briefed spaces is typically 20% for this building type (net:gross ratio = 80%) – this figure has been used to calculate the gross area (above), on which the construction cost estimate is based.		The benchmark sq metre rate for this building type is £1,350. A higher quality is expected and for budget purposes the rate has been increased slightly.		The high-level estimate of the construction cost without considering any site-specifc costs.

requirements set out in the Initial Project Brief are coordinated with the contents of the Project Budget and that they are satisfied with both prior to Stage 2 commencing.

How do Feasibility Studies influence the preparation of the Initial Project Brief?

A core theme in this chapter is the holistic consideration of any aspect that might impact on the preparation of the Concept Design. On a greenfield site there may be less of a need to undertake Feasibility Studies; however, on a constrained urban site, such studies may be essential to ensure that the areas and relationships required by the client can be achieved. There is, of course, a fine line between volumetric studies that ratify the Initial Project Brief and the commencement of a Concept Design. Feasibility Studies should be less design orientated and geared towards testing the brief.

On certain projects, particularly larger and more complex ones, a client adviser (CA) can produce any Feasibility Studies that are necessary and can also assist in the briefing process. The use of a CA helps to ensure that such studies are prepared only for briefing purposes; a CA is less likely to step over the line and stray into Stage 2 activities and the preparation of the Concept Design.

The lead designer's interest in any Feasibility Studies is in ensuring that the Initial Project Brief and the site are aligned and that any potential anomalies have been flagged up, solutions agreed and, where necessary, the Initial Project Brief adjusted.

Example of Feasibility Study

Most hotel operators have standard room layouts that have been fine-tuned over many years to reflect their brand and meet their specific business model requirements. They also tend to operate with a standard number of 'keys' (rooms), which they know their business plan and back and front-of-house activities (reception, linen rooms etc) can support. However, the shape of a given site will not always align with such requirements and cannot be altered. Feasibility Studies at Stage 1 can be essential for demonstrating to an operator that a site is capable of accommodating their brief.

What would a Site Information review consider at Stage 1?

Good quality Site Information is a core project requirement from the lead designer's perspective. At Stage 1, a digital topographical site survey may be required in order to facilitate any Feasibility Studies. Of greater importance is to consider what Site Information will be required at the beginning of Stage 2. Much of this information will need to be tendered, commissioned and produced by specialist survey companies, or researched by utility companies, therefore it is essential to consider the requirements early in Stage 1 to ensure the requisite information can be delivered for the commencement of Stage 2. Site Information might comprise:

I topographical information
I existing building information
I utilities survey
I trees survey
I historical facts and data.

In some circumstances, for example where a client has an option on a site pending planning consent, some surveys will be postponed until a later stage. In this example, it is possible that the Planning Application will be made at the end of Stage 2; however, there are risks associated with this approach (these are discussed in the next chapter). As part of their risk assessment, the lead designer needs to consider the risks of having limited Site Information at Stage 2 and must convey these to the client accordingly.

What procurement activities are necessary at Stage 1?

Stage 1 procurement activities are driven by a core decision made at Stage 0: whether the Concept Design is to be led by the lead designer or by the contractor. In both scenarios it is important that the project lead prepares the Project Roles Table and Contractual Tree, as set out below, so that it is clear what parties are required at each stage and who will be responsible for appointing them. The activities at Stage 1 will be as follows:

| Contractor-led team
   1. Prequalification documentation is issued by the client or project lead (on public sector projects, *OJEU* processes will need to be adhered to).
   2. Interested contractors respond, submissions are vetted and a tender list is determined.
   3. Information Exchanges are prepared, bearing in mind that increased robustness is required as this information will be incorporated into the Employer's Requirements (see page 46).
   Employer's Requirements are issued to shortlisted contractors, enabling Stage 2 to commence and each contractor to prepare their Concept Design.

| Lead designer-led team
   1. The client decides if the lead designer will appoint design team or if design team members are to be appointed individually (see Contractual Trees in figures 1.3 and 1.4).
   2. Prequalification documentation is issued (on public sector projects, *OJEU* processes will need to be adhered to).
   3. Interested design teams or design team members respond, submissions are vetted and a tender list is determined.
   4. The procurement route is decided, allowing Schedules of Services and other appointment documents to be prepared accordingly.
   5. Tender documents are issued and following a review of submissions the design team members are appointed prior to Stage 2 commencing.

Procurement route

In the RIBA Plan of Work 2013, procurement generally refers to the procurement of the project team and how the client, contractor and design team will be contractually connected. The procurement route refers to the more specific process of how a contractor will be appointed. The design team will be appointed by the client or the contractor depending on the procurement route. On some procurement routes the design team is novated to the contractor, typically at Stage 3 or 4.

The Project Roles Table and Contractual Tree are crucial tools, which the project lead will have to consider and develop through discussion with the client. These tools ensure that:

| each project team member is identified
| it is clear who is the employer of each project team member
| the structure of the design team is clear
| initial considerations related to specialist consultants are carried out
| it is clear at what stages each project team member will be involved.

The purpose of these two documents is set out in greater detail in *Assembling a Collaborative Project Team* and templates are available in the toolbox on the RIBA Plan of Work 2013 website (www.ribaplanofwork.com).

| Project Roles Table

The Project Roles Table (see figure 1.1) sets out, in a simple diagram, all of the roles required on a project at each stage. It needs to be remembered that a successful project team is built incrementally and then downsized as the design progresses to the construction and in use stages.

If the number of project team members increases too quickly, the lead designer will face significant challenges as each member of the team tries to bring particular points, not relevant to that stage, to their attention. Conversely, if one party is appointed too late, design work that has already been completed may have to be re-evaluated. For example, a fire engineer's input may significantly affect the Concept Design, such as in relation to an atrium or similar space, whereas an

Project Roles Table

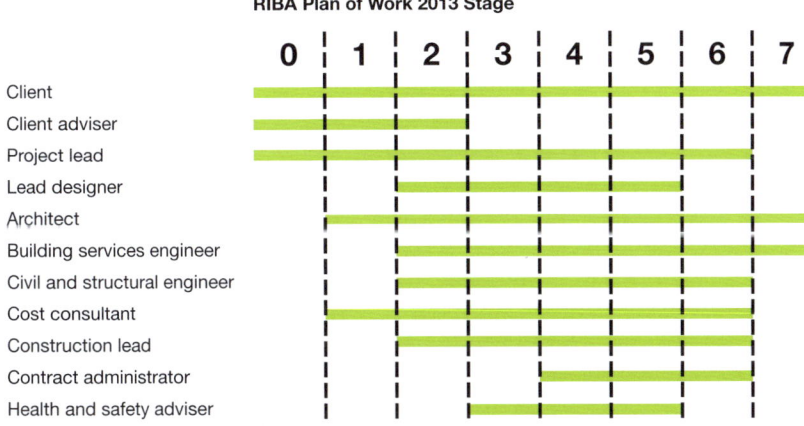

Figure 1.1   Example of a Project Roles Table

acoustician's input may not be required until Stage 3, or even Stage 4, depending on the nature of the project.

Contractual Tree

The Project Roles Table and Contractual Tree have been created as different documents because the same Project Roles Table can result in different Contractual Trees. For example, the building services engineer might be employed by the client, the architect or the contractor. Figures 1.2 to 1.4 have been prepared on the basis of the Project Roles Table in figure 1.1 but illustrate how different procurement routes contractually connect the different project team members in different ways.

The Contractual Tree and Project Roles Table fundamentally frame the preparation of the more detailed Design Responsibility Matrix, Information Exchanges and Schedules of Services that will be included in the tender documents for the professional services of the design team.

From the lead designer's perspective, the Contractual Tree may dictate that members of the design team are determined and appointed by

Contractual Trees

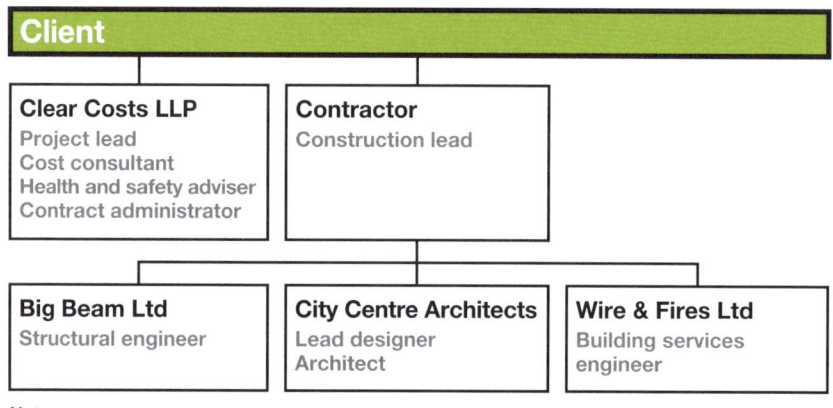

Notes:

1 The contract administrator role is the Employer's Agent for a JCT project.

2 The lead designer might employ the structural or building services engineer as an alternative to this diagram.

Figure 1.2   Contractor-led team

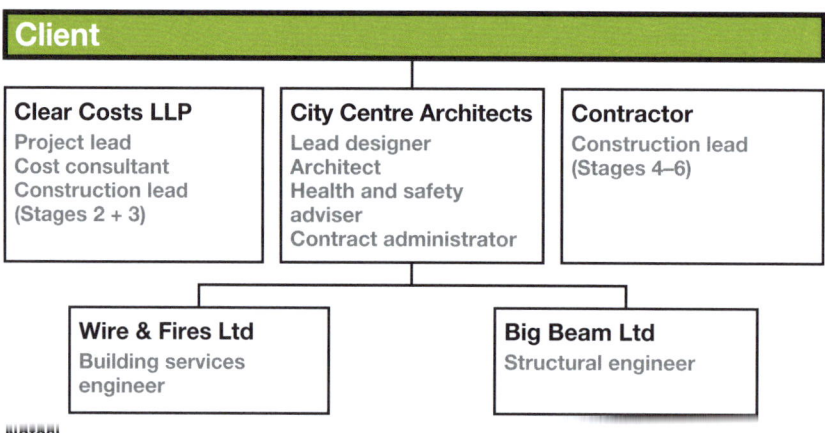

Notes:

1 Traditional procurement route is being used in this example.

2 The Cost Consultant practice is undertaking the construction lead role in the early stages with the architectural practice undertaking the health and safety adviser role. This is based on their internal specialisms and experience.

3 This form of diagram can be used for most forms of procurement in the early stages. On design and build forms of procurement the design team may be novated to the contractor for Stage 4.

Figure 1.3   Lead designer-led design team

Contractual Trees (*continued*)

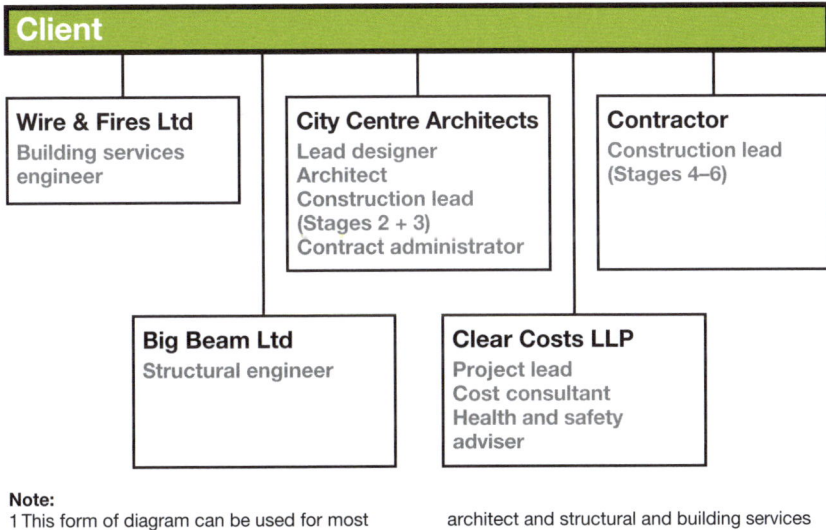

Note:
1 This form of diagram can be used for most forms of procurement in the early stages. On design and build forms of procurement the architect and structural and building services engineer may be novated to the contractor for Stage 4 (see figure 1.3).

Figure 1.4   Design team appointed independently

others. This can present significant risks where the lead designer has no experience of working with the selected design team, and while the client and project lead may consider that lower fees might be obtained by tendering each design team appointment separately, it may result in the creation of a dysfunctional design team. In contrast, a design team assembled by the lead designer is likely to contain members who have worked together on many occasions and have already established collaborative working methods and relationships. The lead designer needs to be mindful of the different risks presented by these very different models and their associated Contractual Trees.

It is advantageous for the project lead to include the Project Roles Table with the tender documents for selecting the design team, so that the lead designer can comment strategically and be satisfied that the right parties will be contributing to the design process at the right time.

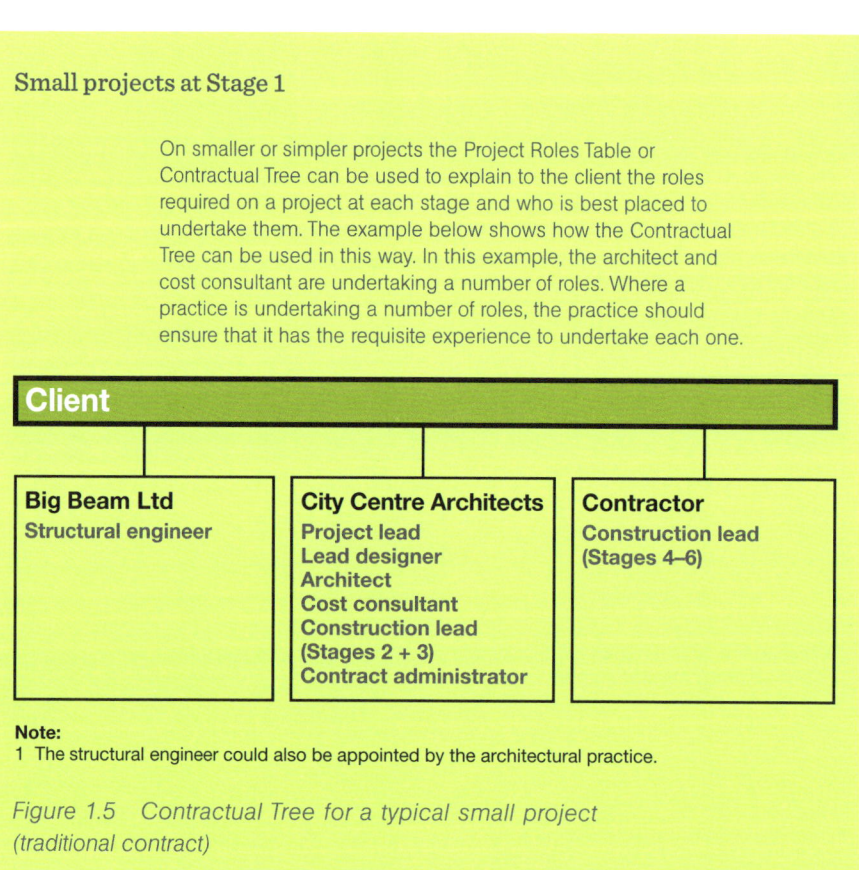

Small projects at Stage 1

On smaller or simpler projects the Project Roles Table or Contractual Tree can be used to explain to the client the roles required on a project at each stage and who is best placed to undertake them. The example below shows how the Contractual Tree can be used in this way. In this example, the architect and cost consultant are undertaking a number of roles. Where a practice is undertaking a number of roles, the practice should ensure that it has the requisite experience to undertake each one.

Client

| **Big Beam Ltd**
Structural engineer | **City Centre Architects**
Project lead
Lead designer
Architect
Cost consultant
Construction lead
(Stages 2 + 3)
Contract administrator | **Contractor**
Construction lead
(Stages 4–6) |

Note:
1 The structural engineer could also be appointed by the architectural practice.

Figure 1.5   Contractual Tree for a typical small project (traditional contract)

By the end of Stage 1 the design team (or design teams in the event of contractor-led procurement) will be in place and each designer will have clear and unambiguous responsibilities for the three design stages: Stages 2, 3 and 4. While procurement of the design team is complete at Stage 1, procurement activities will continue during Stages 2, 3 and 4, depending on the procurement route and the timing of concluding and signing the Building Contract.

Who would undertake the lead designer role?

On the vast majority of projects the architect will act as the lead designer. On projects where another designer's tasks predominate then that designer may be the lead designer. For example, the lead designer on a data centre might be the mechanical and electrical (M&E) services engineer, or it might be the civil engineer on a bridge.

On small projects, roles are aggregated and it is likely that the architect would act as the lead designer, although the role may not be identified as such. On larger projects it is common for professional services contracts to be put out for tender with the lead designer and architect roles combined. Exceptions to this are where tenders are requested for a design team. In both circumstances it would be common for an architectural practice to perform both roles.

What would the lead designer do?

It is important to distinguish between the role of the lead designer and that of a design manager. A design manager is responsible for managing the direction of the design process, putting in place procedures specific to the design process and undertaking progress reviews as design progresses whereas the lead designer is required to make design decisions and direct the design process. A design manager needs to understand the iterative nature of the design process and the tools that can assist this. Depending on their skill sets, they may also review the drawings that are produced.

As the lead designer is a core design role it is important that a designer undertakes this role. The reason that the lead designer and architect roles are frequently amalgamated is that there is an extremely close relationship between the two. One way of defining the difference between the two roles would be to think of them in the following way: the architect is the designer who creates the overall vision and concept for a project, and the lead designer ensures that the work of the other designers (design team members) is successfully incorporated into this vision. Even if two individuals or teams from the same practice are undertaking these roles, there needs to be a very close and exemplar working relationship between the two for a project to be successful. Of course, the same principle applies between all design and project team members, hence the push for collaborative working methods.

Why is the Project Programme crucial at Stage 1?

As outlined in chapter 1, the Project Programme can be a core strategic document. It is at the heart of collaborative contracts, such as PPC2000, and as such it is an essential document at Stage 1. The RIBA Plan of Work 2013 requires a review of the Project Programme at Stage 1. Although the periods are fundamentally set out at Stage 0, they will be imbedded into the professional services contracts at Stage 1. It is essential that the detailed timescales are considered by the project lead, who will prepare the Project Programme.

One concern for the lead designer is that the periods allocated for the core design stages (Stages 2, 3 and 4) are likely to be set in the Project Programme at Stage 1 without their input. Those responsible for preparing the Project Programme should have the requisite experience and be confident that the time frames available for each stage are sufficient for the size and complexity of the project. However, the lead designer should contribute to the development of the Project Programme and be satisfied with its contents prior to being appointed. Where possible, this should be undertaken in discussion with the other members of the design team. The Project Programme:

l   sets out the overall project timescale from the commencement of Stage 0 until the end of Stage 6 (Stage 7 activities would be included in a separate programme)
l   establishes the periods of time for each of the design stages (Stages 2, 3 and 4)
l   includes the period for construction and post-occupancy activities
l   determines the periods and timing for client sign-off
l   clarifies when the planning application will be submitted, and
l   considers the extent to which certain stages will overlap.

In contributing to, or commenting on, the Project Programme the lead designer should use their experience to comment on the periods of time allocated for each design stage and provide opinion on risks that may be generated by overlapping stage periods with approval periods (planning consent, for example) or other activities. Where a risk has been identified it is essential that the implications are managed in a fair and reasonable manner. This is of particular importance if the team is being assembled to work collaboratively. For example, if the programme dictates that the design team has to commence Stage 4 work prior to the granting of planning consent, it is only fair that the client accepts this risk and recompenses the design team in the event that the planning process requires changes to the design.

Example of a Project Programme for a simple project

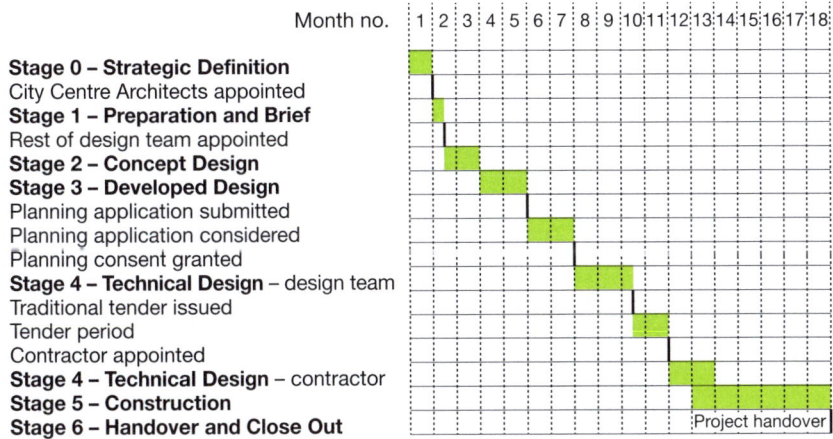

Figure 1.6   Example of a Project Programme for a simple project

How might town planning influence Stage 1?

The RIBA Plan of Work 2013 requires 'Pre-application discussions' to take place during Stage 1. As the design team has not been appointed at Stage 1, the following parties may be present at a meeting with the local planners:

I   the client
I   the project lead
I   a client adviser
I   a planning consultant.

Any feedback from discussions can be incorporated into the Initial Project Brief to allow the design team to act accordingly during Stage 2, although such feedback is likely to be non-binding and the lead designer should consider very carefully how to manage any comments that are raised and how to deal with them during Stage 2. For example, during initial discussions the planners may state preferences in relation to materials that are acceptable and these preferences are then included in the Initial Project Brief. The architect may prefer not to accept these as a given and may wish to determine their rationale and logic before committing to such restraints on their design. On smaller projects it is usual that the architect will liaise with the planners at every stage; it is likely that the architect will have local knowledge and established relationships with the local planning authority and so will understand what is likely to be acceptable or unacceptable to them without the need for pre-application discussions.

What supporting tasks should be undertaken during Stage 1?

The Suggested Key Support Tasks at Stage 1 comprise the following:

I Prepare Handover Strategy and Risk Assessments.
I Agree Schedule of Services, Design Responsibility Matrix and Information Exchanges and prepare Project Execution Plan including Technology and Communication Strategies and consideration of Common Standards to be used.

The Suggested Key Support Tasks noted in the RIBA Plan of Work 2013 have been devised to support the Core Objectives and to ensure that the documentation required to assemble the project team, as set out in the Procurement task bar activities, is prepared.

What is the purpose of the Handover Strategy?

The Handover Strategy reflects the increasing complexity of handing over a building at Practical Completion. A number of detailed tasks need to be undertaken as construction nears an end. The mechanical and electrical systems need to be commissioned. Users need to be trained on how to use the systems within the building (even residential projects use increasingly complex controls) or guided on how passive environmental measures should be used if they are to achieve the expected Project Outcomes. The increasing requirement on more complex projects for seasonal commissioning creates further challenges. Most importantly, if Stage 7 of the RIBA Plan of Work 2013 is to be harnessed effectively, operational requirements must be defined in the briefing stages as well as the information that will be required for use in any computer-aided facilities management (CAFM) software.

Handover strategy

More on this subject can be gleaned by examining BSRIA's Soft Landings guidance (www.bsria.co.uk/services/design/soft-landings/free-guidance/), and for those undertaking government projects it is also useful to consider the government's Soft Landings approach (www.bimtaskgroup.org/gsl/).

How might the lead designer contribute to Risk Assessments?

The Risk Assessments referred to in the RIBA Plan of Work 2013 do not specifically refer to assessments that might be undertaken to comply with health and safety legislation, although such assessments may be included. The project lead needs to consider at Stage 1 any aspects that may impact on or be a risk to the design process at Stage 2. Examples might include:

l concerns about road access complying with local authority highway department requirements
l the availability of sufficient utilities
l conditions that may be imposed by local planners.

Some risks may be identified as being potential 'showstoppers' – these will require further investigation by the project lead and discussions and agreement with the client. For example, a drainage or power network may be close to capacity, requiring an expensive solution – either an expansion of the network or the provision of a connection well outside the site boundary. As long as the risks have been identified and accepted by the client, the project can proceed to Stage 2 when they can be examined in greater detail.

At the commencement of Stage 2 the lead designer needs to consider any risks (particularly design risks) that have been identified and come to their own views on these as well as considering if any additional risks exist. During Stage 2 the project lead will continue to identify, record, manage and eliminate holistic project risks using a separate risk register. Such risks would include:

l aspects of the fire engineering strategy requiring further negotiations with local authority, such as the extent of sprinkler provision

I   utilities aspects outside the site, for example, the need for new substations or a new water main to serve the site

I   the scope of contributions required from the local authority or utility providers, which may impact on the Business Case.

The next chapter considers the design status schedule and how it can successfully be used to manage and mitigate design risks during the design stages. The management of design risks should be transferred to the lead designer once they have been appointed.

Why are the Schedules of Services, Design Responsibility Matrix and Information Exchanges crucial to the lead designer's role?

Careful consideration and preparation of the Schedules of Services, Design Responsibility Matrix and Information Exchanges for inclusion in the professional services contracts for the design team is one of the most important tasks for the project lead during Stage 1. The issues associated with this have already been considered and the lead designer needs to be satisfied that the documents are all acceptable before proceeding to Stage 2.

In scenarios where a lead designer-led team is being tendered, the project lead may include the Information Exchanges in the tender documents, leaving the Design Responsibility Matrix to be prepared by the lead designer in conjunction with their design team. In such circumstances the project lead may wish to include the Stage 4 design responsibilities, so that the expected boundaries between the design team and the specialist subcontractors are clear.

Templates for all of the tools covered in this section are available at www. ribaplanofwork.com and further guidance is available in *Assembling a Collaborative Project Team*.

Design Responsibility Matrix

Design and management responsibilities are crucial subjects as they fundamentally frame the fees set by the design team. The Design Responsibility Matrix defines the design interfaces between members of the design team and also the interfaces between the design team and any specialist subcontractors appointed by the contractor. These boundaries will be relevant regardless of the chosen procurement route, which establishes more holistic contractual responsibilities. The project lead should be satisfied that they have, or have appointed those who do have, the experience and skills required to prepare this schedule. At present, no sector 'norms' are available; however, initiatives are under way to change this. At Stage 2, the lead designer may wish to update the matrix should the Stage 1 schedule not cover a particular aspect of the Concept Design.

The Design Responsibility Matrix can be prepared as a 'project' version, to meet the needs of a particular project. Alternatively, a 'practice' version can be prepared, to be used time and time again, although this may require tweaking to suit a particular project; for example, to include any additional or new design team members required to meet the specific demands of a project.

Small projects at Stage 1

The Design Responsibility Matrix is of greatest benefit when more than one party will be carrying out design duties, and particularly when different practices are working together for the first time. On small projects, where the designers may have worked together many times before, a 'practice' version can still be useful, bringing clarity in the event of a dispute. The matrix can also be used to clarify, as part of any fee proposals, any design aspects that will be concluded by a specialist subcontractor as part of the Building Contract (Contractor's Designed Portion in JCT contracts). From the lead designer's point of view, it brings clarity on who will do what, when, providing comfort that the information required to satisfactorily conclude coordination and integration exercises will be available at the right time and is included within the fees of each design team member.

Why is the Design Responsibility Matrix crucial to the lead designer?

The Design Responsibility Matrix is a new project tool in the RIBA Plan of Work 2013. Schedules of Services have historically been prepared for each design team member individually, with some tasks inevitably falling into the cracks between the different schedules. The Design Responsibility Matrix addresses this by covering each aspect of the

A completed Stage 2 Design Responsibility Matrix

Element	Design responsibility	Level of detail	Level of information	
Substructure	C&S engineer	2	2	
Frame/upper slabs - steel	C&S engineer	2	2	
Fire protection	Architect	2	2	
Stairs (precast)	C&S engineer	2	2	
Brickwork/blockwork	Architect	2	2	
Masonry support	C&S engineer	2	2	
Curtain walling	Architect	3	2	
Insulated render	Architect	2	2	
Stone cladding	Architect	3	2	
Louvres	Architect	2	2	
Ceiling systems	Architect	2	2	
Hot and cold water services	M&E engineer	2	2	
Ventilation (natural and a/c)	M&E engineer	3	2	
Sprinklers	M&E engineer	2	2	
Electrical services	M&E engineer	2	2	
Lifts	M&E engineer	2	2	

Notes:

1   The example above looks solely at Stage 2. A completed Design Responsibility Matrix (DRM) for Stages 2, 3 and 4 should be completed at Stage 1 for incorporating into the professional services contracts.

2   The Stage 3 section of the DRM would be similar to that for Stage 2, reflecting the increased level of model definition (a combination of LOD and LOI) taking place during this stage. The Stage 4 DRM needs to look at the boundaries between the design team and the specialist subcontractors. A Stage 4 DRM is illustrated in figure 4.1.

3   Classification references are not shown. It is anticipated that these will be developed 'below the bonnet' with mapping between systems, such as Uniclass, Omniclass and NRM, allowing greater use of the terms above for different purposes until a common classification system is developed.

4   A notes column would be added to the completed DRM to allow a finer granularity. For example, for ceiling systems it might show the architect as responsible with the M&E engineer providing supporting advice and contributory information, such as lighting, sprinkler head or smoke detector positions. The design responsibility column may also be bolstered by adding a column that defines

support roles. This would be of particular use on the largest of projects.

5   In the example above several items are showing as having an enhanced LOD for the stage (LOD3). This may be the result of a client's specific requirements or perhaps the lead designer requires an enhancement of LOD in order to design to cost.

6   **Level of detail (LOD)**

LOD in the 'analogue' version of the DRM in *Assembling a Collaborative Project Team* used scale. Initiatives to shift LOD and LOI to a 'digital' format are under way and will be published in the spring of 2015. Updates will be available at www.nbs.com, where the attributes for this column will be considered in greater detail. LOD primarily relates to geometry and this initiative will provide clarity on what the appropriate LOD for each project stage should be. For the purposes of this example, LOD 2 is defined as the level of detail suitable for a RIBA Stage 2 Concept Design.

7   **Level of information (LOI)**

LOI primarily relates to the specification and data. LOI 2 is defined as the level of detail suitable for a RIBA Stage 2 Concept Design. The ability to edit the LOI acknowledges that the descriptive to prescriptive journey varies depending on sector, client or other factors.

Figure 1.7   Extract from a completed Design Responsibility Matrix (incorporating Information Exchanges) showing Stage 2 responsibilities

building in a multidisciplinary way. Any issues can be addressed before the design team is appointed and design work progresses, minimising the risk of disruption during the design process. Because the matrix also addresses the interfaces between the design team and any specialist subcontractors, the Building Contract, regardless of procurement route, will acknowledge this crucial interface. The lead designer will then be clear from the outset about the expectations for each designer, particularly at Stage 4, where these may be ambiguous. By addressing these complex interfaces prior to Stage 2 commencing, the lead designer can focus on coordinating and integrating the work of each designer, rather than resolving issues associated with who does what and when. Put another way, the Design Responsibility Matrix ensures the right information is produced at the right time by the right designer.

What might the lead designer add to the Project Execution Plan?

The Project Execution Plan is a crucial document from the lead designer's perspective. It is also fundamental to assembling a collaborative project team.

The project lead may use a 'light touch' at Stage 1 to ensure that core requirements, such as meeting frequencies and locations, are incorporated allowing sufficient flexibility for the lead designer to expand on the design management aspects at Stage 2. In some instances the information required from the design team, such as the Technology Strategy, will be requested during the tender process for professional services.

The Technology Strategy sets out the hardware and software that will be used by the project team members and, more importantly, considers the format of output files to be produced by each party. The lead designer needs to ensure that all members of the design team contribute to this strategy and are content that the output produced by one party can be imported into their own software packages. Despite a move towards interoperability standards (IFCs) more work is required before the importing and exporting of files from one software package to another is seamless. This particular subject therefore requires close attention from the lead designer to avoid a situation downstream when one designer is unable to progress due to software incompatibility issues.

The Communication Strategy contained in the Project Execution Plan is most likely to be set by the project lead. However, the lead designer will need to contribute to any aspects of the strategy that impact on the design process; for example, while video conferencing can assist communication, it might not be suitable for design discussions.

Setting Common Standards on a project from the outset, to help facilitate a collaborative team, is a new but emerging concept. Until such standards have been fully developed, embraced and adopted, those undertaking the project lead and lead designer roles should be mindful of developments and their uptake and success.

Why are Sustainability Checkpoints important?

A Core Objective during Stage 1 is to define the Sustainability Aspirations. These should be considered by the project team in conjunction with the client and included in the Initial Project Brief.

The Sustainability Checkpoints provide straightforward guidance on the key sustainability tasks to be undertaken at a particular stage. The lead designer's interest is primarily related to ensuring that these tasks are carried out and that there are no requirements in the Initial Project Brief that may contradict them. The checkpoints included in the RIBA Plan of Work 2013 are set out in greater detail in the digital version of the RIBA Plan of Work 2013 at www.ribaplanofwork.com.

What are the Stage 1 Information Exchanges?

The Information Exchanges at Stage 1 are:

- Initial Project Brief
- Project Budget
- Feasibility Studies
- Site Information
- Project Roles Table and Contractual Tree
- Project Programme
- Handover Strategy
- Risk Assessments
- Schedules of Services
- Design Responsibility Matrix incorporating Information Exchanges
- Project Execution Plan.

This information can be grouped into two categories:

I the information required to successfully facilitate the Stage 2 Concept Design process
I the information required to successfully appoint the project team to ensure that the right information is prepared at the right time.

Chapter summary   1

This chapter has demonstrated that many of the tasks undertaken during Stage 1 are of importance to the lead designer. The Initial Project Brief, Project Budget and Feasibility Studies need to be coordinated and any contradictory or conflicting aspects resolved if the design team is to be successful at Stage 2. Similarly, if the Project Roles Table, Contractual Tree, Design Responsibility Matrix and other documents included in the professional services contracts have not been considered properly, problems will arise during the design stages. A major conundrum identified is that the lead designer is not appointed during Stage 1. This requires the project lead to have or acquire the skills required to produce robust documentation and, of course, the lead designer should make certain that any documentation is acceptable before being appointed and proceeding to Stage 2.

Concept Design

Chapter overview

Stage 2 is a crucial stage for the lead designer. A Concept Design that meets the Initial Project Brief must be developed by the architect and this design must be presented and accepted by the client and other stakeholders. During the stage the lead designer must direct the work of the other design team members and incorporate their work into the developing Concept Design. The management of the many, often conflicting, inputs into the iterative design process make this the most challenging of the design stages. An inspiring Concept Design can motivate the project team, but it will only act as a good springboard into Stage 3 if the lead designer has successfully directed and managed the incorporation of strategic coordination issues.

The key coverage in this chapter is as follows:

What are the Core Objectives of Stage 2?

How do procurement activities influence the lead designer's role?

What influences the Project Programme at Stage 2?

How does town planning influence design management at Stage 2?

What supporting tasks should be undertaken during Stage 2?

What Information Exchanges are common at Stage 2?

Introduction

The lead designer is typically not appointed until Stage 2. Before this stage commences, it is essential that the lead designer reviews the outputs prepared at Stage 1 (likely as part of their appointment process). Of particular interest should be the Project Programme, the Project Execution Plan, the Design Responsibility Matrix and the Information Exchanges, which were all considered in the previous chapter. The lead designer should be satisfied that all of these documents are in order and, if necessary, request alterations that enable the services to be performed as envisaged.

The architect has a crucial role at Stage 2, and from a design perspective Stage 2 is the most important project stage. The Initial Project Brief must be interpreted and ideas developed, according to the unique aspects of the site, until the bones of a coherent Concept Design that fits onto the chosen site are created. While the core relationship will be between the architect and the client, the lead designer also plays a pivotal role.

With the architect starting the stage with a 'blank' computer screen, the job of the lead designer is to determine when the initial concept ideas are robust enough, and the client sufficiently comfortable with them, to justify the involvement of the other design team members. The challenges for the lead designer associated with this simple premise can be considerable. Whatever design management tools and techniques are used, the lead designer must orchestrate the production of adequate and robust overlays by the other design team members during the stage to demonstrate that the architect's Concept Design is robust and ready to proceed to Stage 3.

Some architects may require specific advice in the early stages to assist the development of the Concept Design. This is obviously acceptable, although it makes sense for the lead designer to monitor such developments.

The lead designer's role during this stage is to manage the work of the design team and ensure that the right information is provided at the right time. A careful balance needs to be struck. Too many strategic coordination exercises may impede the design process, particularly if the client is still not convinced by a particular proposal, but too few may result in a Concept Design that is not sufficiently thought through and which requires substantial alterations at Stage 3, when the coordination work begins in earnest. An experienced lead designer will know which items need to be addressed and which might reasonably be left until the next stage, if necessary.

What are the Core Objectives of this stage?

The Core Objectives of the RIBA Plan of Work 2013 at Stage 2 are:

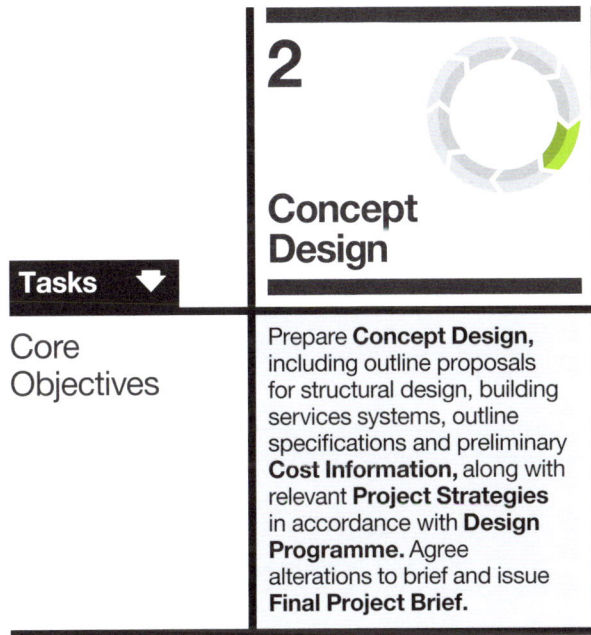

2

Concept Design

Tasks ▼

Core Objectives

Prepare **Concept Design,** including outline proposals for structural design, building services systems, outline specifications and preliminary **Cost Information,** along with relevant **Project Strategies** in accordance with **Design Programme.** Agree alterations to brief and issue **Final Project Brief.**

The Core Objectives of Stage 2 revolve around the creation of an exciting and robust Concept Design. The Concept Design acts as a bridge between the client's brief, the planning process, the site and the architect's vision, and sows the seeds for the other design stages that will be essential before construction commences. It is arguable that the greatest value is achieved during Stage 2, with the Developed Design (Stage 3) proving the robustness of the Concept Design and ironing out any loose edges, and the Technical Design (Stage 4) allowing sufficient information for construction (and increasingly, for In Use purposes) and, depending on the procurement route used, for enabling the contractor to calculate a lump sum cost or other tender sum.

For the Concept Design to be robust it must be aligned with the outline proposals for the structural engineering design and building services systems and the outline specifications from all of the designers. The design information must be aligned with the preliminary Cost Information, and it may also be essential to have a number of Project Strategies which support the design and Cost Information. A Design Programme is essential during this stage, although there a number of challenges associated with preparing this, which are considered below. It may also be necessary to review the brief as the Concept Design develops – a Final Project Brief that is consistent with the Concept Design and Cost Information is a core Information Exchange at the end of the stage.

While the architect is wrestling with initial conceptual ideas, the lead designer has, in parallel, a number of essential tasks that need to be undertaken. These include:

I developing a Design Programme
I holding initial meetings with the design team
I initiating a process for recording agreed changes to the Initial Project Brief
I considering revisions to the Project Execution Plan.

Before considering the tasks carried out in Stage 2, and their importance to the lead designer, it is essential to remember that the design process is iterative, requiring inputs (comments) from the client and other stakeholders as the design progresses. Also, due to the considerable and varying dynamics between the various parties and the many individual aspects of any project, Stage 2 is likely to completed in a unique way on every project. The lead designer must, therefore, adopt a flexible approach, using programming techniques and other design management tools to positively steer the design in the right direction, despite the apparent volatility of the design process.

What are the outline proposals from the other members of the design team?

The outline proposals from the other design team members at Stage 2 should consider the core coordination aspects of the project. For example:

I What is the main structural grid? Is it robust? Are there sector considerations? What is the best material for the frame (steel, concrete, timber)? What aspects would drive this decision? It is not necessary or feasible to resolve every structural beam size during the stage.
I What are the core building services systems in the building. What risers and plant rooms are required to accommodate them?

❙ What is the proposed floor-to-floor height of the building. Has this been tested against the architectural concepts (floor zones, ceiling heights, stair concepts) and the structural and building services concepts?

❙ Are there any coordination aspects that might impact on the core spatial arrangements? For example, do adjacent building heights act as a constraint on floor-to-floor heights?

As well as considering these core issues, some concepts may require specific and essential inputs from other design team members at Stage 2. For example, road junction designs may be needed from the highway engineer to enable parking exercises to be undertaken. The lead designer needs to make sure that the Project Roles Table is adjusted for such inputs if they were not anticipated during Stage 1.

In summary, the amount of coordination undertaken at Stage 2 will vary from project to project. The purpose of coordination undertaken during this stage is to ensure that the Concept Design is sufficiently robust that when the core and more detailed coordination exercises are undertaken at Stage 3 they do not require a fundamental re-evaluation of the Concept Design.

Why is the outline specification important?

The outline specification, required as part of the Concept Design, connects many aspects of the design process at Stage 2. Therefore, from the lead designer's perspective, it is an important tool and a core project document. For example, the specification:

❙ is intrinsically linked to costs
❙ enables the lead designer to consider initial aspects of coordination
❙ communicates finishes and other items to the client.

Like the coordination exercises, the outline specification does not need to drill too deeply into every item at Stage 2. For example, the construction cost estimate may not be sensitive to the WC or toilet cubicle specification at Stage 2, but whether the elevations use stone, render or a customised curtain walling system will have a major impact. The level of contingency allocated at this stage is crucial as it must recognise that the specification will be refined during Stage 3. The lead designer needs to prioritise specification issues that might impact on cost during this stage, and must also focus on any aspects that are not incorporated within the design proposals but might commonly be required. For example, dock levellers might typically be required in a loading bay but not drawn at this early stage. The lead designer needs to sure that they are included in the outline specification and, in turn, the construction cost estimate.

What Cost Information is required at Stage 2?

In the previous chapter the items that might inform the development of Cost Information at Stage 1 were considered. At Stage 2, the main cost activity is the preparation of the construction cost estimate based on the Concept Design information. The importance of predicting the likely area of the building during Stage 1 has already been emphasised. At Stage 2, the areas derived from the Concept Design can be used and compared with the metrics used at Stage 1 (the net:gross area ratio, for example).

It needs to be remembered that the Concept Design at Stage 2 starts as a 'blank screen' and that it is likely to be well into the Stage 2 design before the cost consultant can start crunching numbers. With significant iterations of the design possible during this stage, the timing for producing the first cost estimate needs to be carefully considered. The conundrum is that this estimate may reveal that the proposals are not affordable. The challenge for the lead designer and cost consultant during this stage is how to 'design to cost' rather than 'cost the design'. In the latter scenario, the cost consultant costs the draft stage output. However, without any cost exercises having taken place during the design process, it is probable that the design will be over budget and require further iterations. In the former scenario, proactive cost exercises are undertaken to ensure that the proposals meet the client's Project Budget at the end of the stage.

Designing to cost requires a high degree of coordination, cooperation and collaboration between the lead designer, the design team members and the cost consultant. Activities that can assist a 'designing to cost' approach include:

I using cost benchmark information from previous projects
I commencing the elemental cost analysis for key aspects early
I agreeing areas of risk and focusing cost exercises on these areas.

Of course, as cost estimating software integrates more closely with 3D modelling packages, it will be possible for designers to have 'real time' cost updates. While this information might be raw and require interpretation and adjustment, it will still help to inform the lead designer and steer the designers in the right direction earlier in the design process, resulting in fewer iterations and adjustments to the design as it develops.

What is the purpose of Project Strategies?

Project Strategies are a core design management tool and are crucial from the lead designer's perspective. They perform a number of functions, including:

I explaining aspects of the building and/or design proposals that cannot be communicated by drawings or those that require recording for posterity
I allowing the inputs of certain consultants, such as fire engineers or acousticians, to be conveyed in a way that informs the client, other members of the design team or external stakeholders.
I conveying detailed operational strategies to a client for sign-off, such as a security strategy.

The Suggested Key Support Tasks recommend the preparation of a number of core Project Strategies during Stage 2. These include:

I Sustainability Strategy
I Maintenance and Operational Strategy
I Handover Strategy
I Construction Strategy
I Health and Safety Strategy.

These strategies are considered in greater detail below. Other Project Strategies might include:

I a fire engineering strategy
I an acoustic strategy
I a catering strategy
I a security strategy
I an access strategy.

Different parties will produce the various Project Strategies and these responsibilities would be set out in the Schedule of Services at Stage 1. The lead designer would be responsible for reviewing and commenting on them to ensure consistency, resolving any contradictory statements as necessary.

Most Project Strategies have a limited shelf life and very few need to be part of the Information Exchange at Stage 6. Many act as a bridge between the geometry or data aspects required to construct a building or, increasingly, the information used to facilitate better operational or asset management processes while the building is in use. Some focus on a particular aspect that the design must address. For example:

Ι The Construction Strategy interfaces between design and construction, ensuring that buildability is considered as the design develops, as well as interfacing with planning requirements or the logistics associated with a restricted city centre site (requiring just-in-time deliveries).
Ι The Maintenance and Operational Strategy demonstrates how certain aspects of the building will be operated and maintained, such as the lighting in an atrium or lecture theatre.

Project Strategies are crucial from the lead designer's perspective because they clearly communicate the intentions of the design team. It is essential that the lead designer reviews each Project Strategy to identify any areas of conflict or contradictions with other sources of information, including, of course, other Project Strategies. The Project Strategies that have a short shelf life will be replaced by other design information as the project progresses, their communication purpose having been fulfilled. Some Project Strategies, such as the security strategy noted above, may be usefully referenced in the Handover Strategy and will assist the client's facilities management team by concisely setting out the rationale and intentions behind the design.

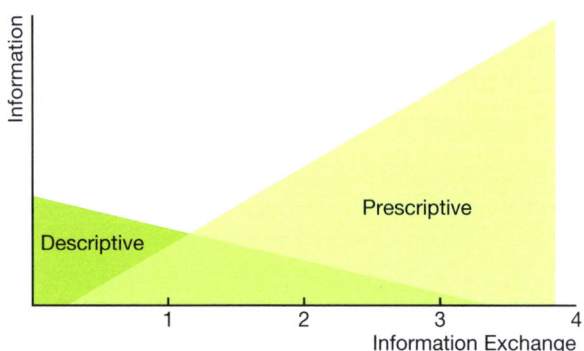

Figure 2.1   Descriptive to prescriptive information journey

The final point to note in relation to Stages 0 to 4 is that project information typically commences in a descriptive form, becoming prescriptive as the design progresses. The Initial Project Brief at Stage 1 describes the client's requirements. The Stage 4 Information Exchanges should all be prescriptive and the information in Stages 2 and 3 somewhere in between as the design progresses and the specification hardens via samples, mock-ups and other means. This descriptive to prescriptive information journey is simply illustrated in figure 2.1.

Why is the Design Programme challenging during Stage 2?

Producing a robust Design Programme for Stage 2 is a significant challenge for the lead designer because many design team activities, which potentially influence each other, need to be undertaken simultaneously. More importantly, and significantly underplayed by those undertaking the lead designer role, design is an iterative process. Due to the substantial number of inputs into the design process it is difficult to predict the number of iterations that will be required before the Concept Design ticks all the boxes. This is particularly the case for third party inputs, which cannot be predicted, controlled or their timing guaranteed, creating further complexities to creating a Design Programme that is robust enough to monitor yet flexible enough to accommodate the iterative process. Figure 2.2 sets out an example of a Stage 2 Design Programme.

Iterative design

In order to progress, construction work has to follow a logical sequence, from the foundations up to the roof finishes. The same principle does not apply to the design process. The inputs to the design process vary, ranging from the client's views and opinions to those of third parties, and to the varying design ideas of the design team. This complexity means that it is inevitable that the design will sometimes have to take one or two steps backwards. Iteration may relate to the work of a designer, particularly the architect at Stage 2, but is of greatest interest to the lead designer, who must marshal and coordinate the design work as it progresses.

Stage 2 Design Programme

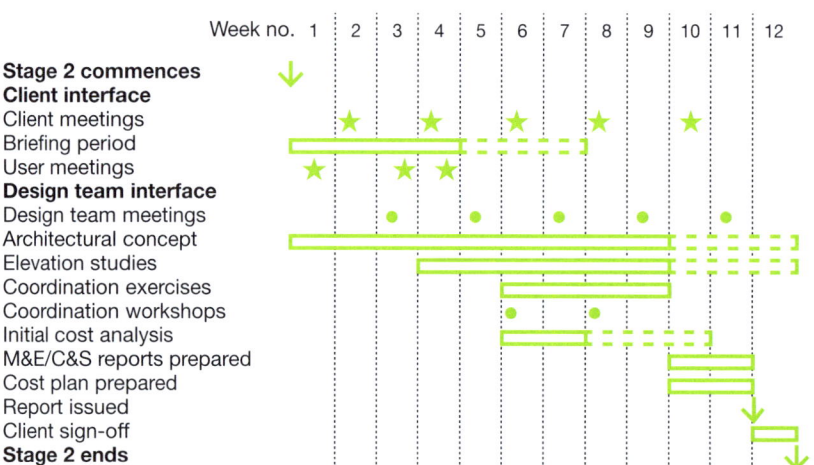

Figure 2.2 Stage 2 Design Programme

The illustrated Design Programme is strategic rather than contractual in its nature and avoids, for example, stating dates for when revisions of the architect's information will be issued and the purposes for which these may be used. This avoids making 'promises' that cannot be delivered. Put another way, the programme shows the general thrust of design activity and focuses on client and other party inputs that would assist the design team in the iterative development of the design. It contains dates of key meetings with the client and would be shared with the client to underline how essential regular contributions to the design process are.

Because the Stage 2 Design Programme needs to be strategic in nature it must be aligned with other design management tools, such as the design status schedule. This will allow the lead designer to properly convey the status of the developing design and to flag up any risks, hot topics or issues that are impeding the design process and the measures being taken to deal with them.

Briefing tracker

Date	Current brief requirement	Proposed change	Status
15-Jan-14	Brief requires 1 no. 400 person lecture theatre.	Space use analysis suggests that 2 no. 200 person lecture spaces would have high utilisation and reduce overall space requirements. Proposal impacts on certain lectures that need to be given twice or electronic teaching tools used to project lecture into second space.	Change agreed by email on 17 Jan with 2 no. 200 person lecture rooms to be incorporated into design in lieu 1 no. 400 person space.
17-Jan-14	Cleaners' cupboards are required for every 1,000 sq. metres of gross space.	Cleaners' cupboards have been included in the architectural layouts. Each cupboard covers 1,200 sq. metres of space but locations work well in layout.	Change agreed (see minutes of 17 Jan design team meeting). Brief superseded by locations on drawings.
17-Jan-14	Tiling required to toilet walls.	Cost consultant concerned that Project Budget cannot accommodate briefing requirement. Painted walls with suitable moisture resistance substrate proposed.	Change agreed – Client agrees that painted walls are acceptable. Verbal instruction on 2 Feb.
02-Feb-14	One brief clause requires a secure site perimeter whereas another asks that the site be open and accessible.	Delete clause from Final Project Brief. Proposals will be incorporated in Concept Design.	Current draft of Final Project Brief incorporates change.

Notes:
1 The Briefing Tracker is not an essential document as long as the Final Project Brief has been revised to ensure that there is nothing that contradicts the Concept Design Proposals. However, on projects with a protracted Stage 2 it is a useful method for capturing and recording decision making that has revolved around the brief.

Figure 2.3   Example of a briefing tracker

While the Feasibility Studies undertaken during Stage 1 contribute towards a more robust Initial Project Brief, it is inevitable that once the Concept Design work begins in earnest, clarifications will be required. Some briefing items will appear ambiguous or contradictory and will need to be reconsidered, whereas other items may require a different design approach. It is therefore important that during Stage 2 any possible changes to the brief are recorded before they are agreed (or not) with the client and then incorporated into the Final Project Brief.

This activity is of paramount importance to the lead designer as it is essential that the Final Project Brief and the Information Exchanges at the end of Stage 2 are fully aligned. The importance of this task will also depend on the role that the brief plays in subsequent stages. For example, on a traditional contract the brief acts as a historical record of decisions that were made, and on a design and build contract it may become a core contract document.

A brief that has a specific purpose beyond Stage 2 will require additional scrutiny. For example, does the Concept Design meet the Quality Objectives, or does the design demonstrate that the Project Outcomes will be achieved? Depending on the responses to these types of questions, the Final Project Brief may need to be adjusted accordingly to avoid conflicting with or contradicting the Concept Design.

How do procurement activities influence the lead designer's role?

With the procurement route agreed at Stage 1, the Project Roles Table and Contractual Tree will remain unaltered during the design stages, although it is possible that the design process may flag up the need for additional project or design team members to provide specific specialist advice. The procurement task bar of the RIBA Plan of Work 2013 contains a 'holding' statement at Stages 2, 3 and 4 as follows:

> The procurement strategy does not fundamentally alter the progression of the design or the level of detail prepared at a given stage. However, **Information Exchanges** will vary depending on the selected procurement route and **Building Contract**. A bespoke **RIBA Plan of Work 2013** will set out the specific tendering and

procurement activities that will occur at each stage in relation to the chosen procurement route.

This text underlines that while the project team members will have been determined at Stage 1, the activities at Stages 2, 3 and 4 continue to respond to the demands of each particular procurement route and when the client and the contractor will enter into and sign a Building Contract. These arrangements will, in turn, impact on the lead designer and the design team. This section sets out the issues that might be encountered and how they are best dealt with. A practice- or project-specific RIBA Plan of Work 2013 generated from www.ribaplanofwork.com will contain generic procurement activities based on the procurement route selected when generating the plan. These activities, as set out in figure 2.4, are focused on each procurement route; however, it is not feasible for the RIBA Plan of Work 2013 to cover the subtle nuances and requirements of every project and client and it is possible that the tasks noted will need to be adjusted to suit a particular project or approach.

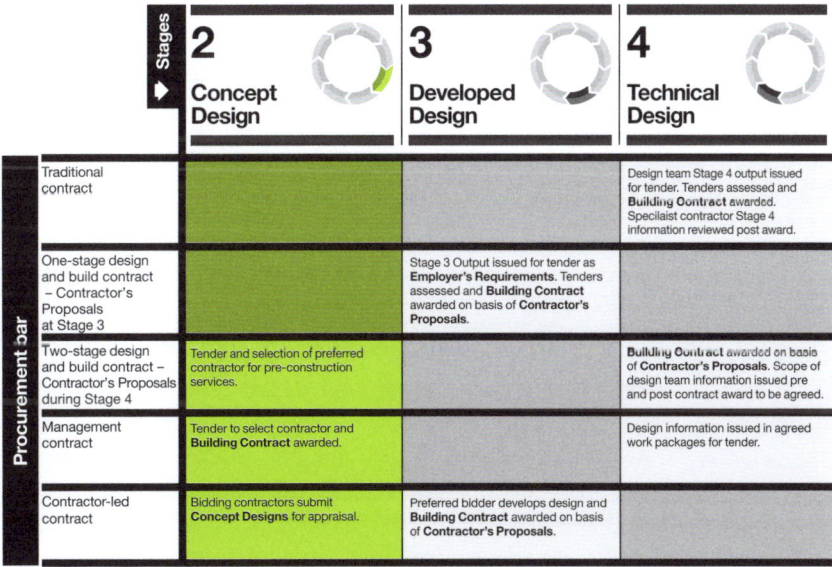

Procurement bar	Stages	2 Concept Design	3 Developed Design	4 Technical Design
	Traditional contract			Design team Stage 4 output issued for tender. Tenders assessed and **Building Contract** awarded. Specialist contractor Stage 4 information reviewed post award.
	One-stage design and build contract – Contractor's Proposals at Stage 3		Stage 3 Output issued for tender as **Employer's Requirements**. Tenders assessed and **Building Contract** awarded on basis of **Contractor's Proposals**.	
	Two-stage design and build contract – Contractor's Proposals during Stage 4	Tender and selection of preferred contractor for pre-construction services.		**Building Contract** awarded on basis of **Contractor's Proposals**. Scope of design team information issued pre and post contract award to be agreed.
	Management contract	Tender to select contractor and **Building Contract** awarded.		Design information issued in agreed work packages for tender.
	Contractor-led contract	Bidding contractors submit **Concept Designs** for appraisal.	Preferred bidder develops design and **Building Contract** awarded on basis of **Contractor's Proposals**.	

Figure 2.4   Procurement activities during Stages 2 to 4 for different procurement routes (Stage 2 highlighted)

Figure 2.4 highlights that at Stage 2, the following procurement activities will take place:

| Management contracting and two-stage design and build procurement
While these are two fundamentally different forms of procurement, the main procurement activity during this stage will be the appointment of a contractor. For both forms of procurement the contractor will be selected following a review of the tender submissions, which will include:
○ rates for prelims, profit and overhead
○ proposed team structure and CVs
○ proposed methodology.
On a management contract the Building Contract will be concluded. On a two-stage design and build contract the contractor will only be appointed to carry out pre-construction services, with the Building Contract being awarded at Stage 4.

From the lead designer's perspective, the main consideration is that both forms of procurement secure the services of the contractor as part of the project team during Stage 2. The contractor will engage in design team meetings and comment on the developing design. The challenge is to ensure that the contractor's contribution is proportionate to the relevance of the stage.

The timing of contractor involvement will vary from project to project. On some projects the tender process may commence at the start of the stage, allowing the contractor to participate in the back end of the Stage 2 design. In other scenarios the Stage 2 Information Exchanges may be included in the tender documents.

| Contractor-led procurement
With contractor-led procurement the Building Contract may be signed at the end of Stage 2 following the review of the various tenders, each with its own Stage 2 Concept Design. However, it is more common for a contract to be signed at the end of Stage 3, allowing a further level of refinement at Stage 3 with a preferred bidder. On a contractor-led project the lead designer and the design team will be appointed by the contractor. As all decision making is done within this integrated team, many aspects of the lead designer's role will be more straightforward; however, the design issues that need to be dealt are likely to be no different. The one point to be mindful of is how communication with

the client should be dealt with, as some contractors may wish to be involved in such dialogue.

What influences the Project Programme at Stage 2?

Even the most robust Project Programme requires tweaking during Stage 2, as the Concept Design develops and some of the likely project risks are examined in greater detail. In addition, discussions with stakeholders, including planners or utility companies, may reveal different timescales to those that were assumed in the Stage 1 Project Programme. The procurement strategy is likely to be formulated in greater detail during this stage and this may also necessitate some fine tuning to the Project Programme.

From the lead designer's perspective, it is essential that any possible changes to the Project Programme identified by the project lead are discussed with the design team and the implications and risks fully considered before any changes are accepted.

How does town planning influence design management at Stage 2?

The RIBA Plan of Work 2013 recommends the submission of a planning application at the end of Stage 3. Some private sector clients require submissions to be made using Stage 2 information. The reasoning behind this is simple: they wish to minimise their costs in scenarios where the certainly of gaining planning consent may not be clear. However, the risks to the lead designer (also acting as the architect in these circumstances) are considerable, and are further compounded as the lead designer is likely to be the only design team member to have been appointed.

It is certainly recommended that those preparing applications using Stage 2 information should be experienced in the sector involved. They should also be able to take a view on the strategic coordination items that other design team members would contribute to, such as structural grids or space requirements for risers and other mechanical and electrical provisions. The Information Exchanges of the architect may also be to a higher level of detail than for a 'typical' Concept Design, particularly in relation to the elevations, and any fee should be considered accordingly. On the basis that it is typical for only the lead designer/architect to be appointed in such scenarios, the implications of submitting a planning application at Stage 2 are not considered further. However, it is suggested that those who do so convey the risks to the client accordingly.

What supporting tasks should be undertaken during Stage 2?

The Suggested Key Support Tasks at Stage 2 comprise the following:

- Prepare Sustainability Strategy, Maintenance and Operational Strategy and review Handover Strategy and Risk Assessments.
- Undertake third party consultations as required and any Research and Development aspects.
- Review and update Project Execution Plan.
- Consider Construction Strategy, including offsite fabrication, and develop Health and Safety Strategy.

At Stage 2 a number of Project Strategies that have already been prepared will be reviewed and updated and new Project Strategies prepared in response to the Concept Design as it progresses. These are summarised below. From a design management perspective, the main point to acknowledge is that certain subjects could be covered in different Project Strategies. For example, both the Sustainability Strategy and the Construction Strategy could address the recycling of waste from site. In such situations, the lead designer should try and keep the text to one document and to include a reference to it in the other. This avoids the potential for conflicting or contradictory text. In this example, it would make more sense for the Construction Strategy to contain the specific information as it is likely that the contractor will prepare and update this strategy and be more influential in the development of this supporting strategy. The Sustainability Strategy can then be worded accordingly.

What is the purpose of the Sustainability Strategy?

The Sustainability Strategy is a crucial document from the lead designer's perspective. It responds to the Sustainability Aspirations set by the client in the Initial Project Brief and should dovetail with the emerging Concept Design. The lead designer's role is to ensure that the client's aspirations are incorporated in the design as it develops. The complexity of this task will depend in part on how detailed the client's aspirations are and how focused the design team is in achieving them. For clients requiring exemplar sustainability outcomes it is essential that the design team is aware of the Sustainability Aspirations from the outset and that the selected team has experience of delivering such expectations.

The Sustainability Aspirations may require a specific BREEAM or LEED rating to be achieved. The lead designer needs to consider early on the rating required and the likelihood of it being achieved. For example, it is more difficult to achieve a higher rating on a out-of-town greenfield site than it is on a city centre brownfield site. Desk-top studies during Stage 2 are therefore an essential part of a holistic design process and will help to ensure that the relevant rating can realistically be achieved.

Why is the Maintenance and Operational Strategy important at Stage 2?

There is a trend for greater emphasis to be placed on the operational aspects of a building. To put it simply, there is no point designing and constructing a building to cost if the costs of maintaining, operating and using it prove to be prohibitive or the building is difficult to maintain. The Maintenance and Operational Strategy allows the design team to demonstrate that such issues have been considered as part of the design process, where they are best integrated into the design proposals. The strategy also ensures that health and safety issues are addressed. At Stage 2, the strategy might consider:

I the architect's proposals for cleaning windows
I the structural engineer's methodology for maintaining exposed steelwork
I the electrical engineer's proposals for replacing lamps in an atrium space
I the mechanical engineer's proposals for replacing plant.

The preparation, checking and development of the Maintenance and Operational Strategy requires good design management skills. It is another core document that should be collated by the lead consultant.

How might the Handover Strategy change at Stage 2?

The Handover Strategy might not change at all during Stage 2. However, it is essential that the lead designer considers its contents alongside the other new and developed Project Strategies and information to ensure that it is up to date.

What influences the Risk Assessments during Stage 2?

Some of the project risks identified during Stage 1 might still exist at the end of Stage 2, although they may have been managed and downgraded. For example, pre-application meetings with planners to discuss the emerging Concept Design may provide greater comfort or provide clarity in relation to areas of concern. More specific discussions and responses from utilities companies may also provide greater certainty in relation to these aspects (for example, that the local high-voltage substation has sufficient capacity to serve the site), but equally they could increase the risk (for example, that the substation does not have sufficient capacity and there will be cost and programme implications for providing extra capacity), requiring particular focus on a certain item.

Many of the new risks identified during Stage 2 will arguably arise from the design process and can be managed using a design status schedule (see below). Certain high-level design risks might be extracted from the design status schedule and incorporated into the project Risk Assessment. Examples might include:

I difficult or potentially expensive utilities connections required outside the site
I the predictability of the local planners' response to a unique design solution
I a core strategy that requires presentation to and sign-off by third parties, such as the fire engineering strategy associated with an atrium.

The difference between risks identified by Risk Assessments and those identified in the design status schedule is simple. The latter are entirely within the control of the design team, whereas the former are risks that the client should be aware of, including those influenced by third parties or any project stakeholder outside the control of the design team.

What third party consultations may be necessary at Stage 2?

For the purposes of the RIBA Plan of Work 2013 a third party is an individual or organisation(s) that is outside the control of the project team (the client, the design team and the contractor). The number of third parties that need to be consulted as a project progresses will vary from project to project, depending on the site context, the scale of the project or the particular sector involved. Third parties might comprise:

I   English Heritage
I   Network Rail
I   Sport England
I   Civil Aviation Authority.

Consents may be required from some third parties, whereas others, such as utility companies, may have to be consulted in order to develop the design proposals. Because third parties are outside the control of the project team they are of great interest to the lead designer. It needs to be considered that:

I   third parties cannot be dictated to, which may impact on the timing and nature of their comments
I   different third parties may have conflicting requirements
I   other projects may have a higher priority
I   as third parties' comments cannot be predicted, they can be extremely disruptive to the design process (unexpected comments at unexpected times can set back the design)
I   third parties can create the biggest project risks because they are outside the client's influence and control.

As well as identifying, in conjunction with the client, project lead and other project team members, any third party that may need to be consulted as the design progresses, the lead designer should ensure that the status of any consultations is adequately represented in:

I   the design status schedule
I   Risk Assessments
I   the stage Design Programme.

Meetings with third parties may be required as part of each consultation process, and some may need to be chased regularly to provide the necessary feedback. Where meetings are organised, they should be incorporated into the Design Programme so that the timing of any possible inputs from a particular third party are understood by the client and the design team.

What Research and Development might be undertaken at Stage 2?

Examples of Research and Development (R&D) undertaken at Stage 2 might include:

I an investigation into a cladding system not previously used by a practice, including a comparison of different systems
I consideration of a new material for integration into an existing cladding system
I research into a subject that may improve the Project Outcomes, such as how design might reduce reoffending in a prison or shorten recovery times in a hospital.

R&D is incorporated into the RIBA Plan of Work 2013 for the first time, acknowledging that it is frequently undertaken on projects for a variety of reasons. The client should be aware of any such research, particularly if it could present a risk to a project. The project lead and/or the lead designer may wish to incorporate aspects of R&D in the Risk Assessments.

In many situations there will be a fine line between what constitutes the Feedback used to inform the Initial Project Brief and what is R&D undertaken by the design team.

How might the Project Execution Plan change at Stage 2?

The Project Execution Plan is a core collaborative tool and as such it should be seen as a live and dynamic, not static, document. At each stage, new parties may join the project team and will need to be added to the plan, which also informs them of the way the project is being managed. Projects can last many years and so new methodologies, software or standards worthy of consideration by the project team may be identified as it progresses. For these reasons there is merit in including 'Project Execution Plan' as an agenda item for project and/or design team meetings. This will ensure that the document is constantly reviewed and updated, as well as underlining its core cultural and procedural purposes. As these same principles apply to the review of the Project Execution Plan at Stages 3, 4 and 5, the document is not considered further in this guide.

Why are Schedules of Services, Design Responsibility Matrix and Information Exchanges considered at Stage 2?

The importance of the Design Responsibility Matrix and Schedules of Services, was mentioned during Stage 1. While these documents will bring greater clarity to who does what and when, it needs to remembered that they are prepared in a vacuum, as no design exists at Stage 1, and therefore there is merit in ensuring that they are updated during Stage 2, so that they remain robust and relevant to the emerging Concept Design.

What should the Construction Strategy consider at this early stage?

During the Concept Design stage there are two drivers for the content of the Construction Strategy: buildability and cost. Needless to say, the Construction Strategy for a low-rise building on a greenfield site might be more straightforward than one for a high-rise building on a constrained city centre site. The types of items that the Construction Strategy might consider include:

- whether a steel, concrete or other structural frame is most appropriate
- what offsite aspects might be of benefit to the project
- logistical issues, such as where site accommodation may be placed on a constrained city centre site or how a narrow staircase will affect operations on a small residential project.

The party appointed to produce the Construction Strategy will vary depending on the project's procurement route and, in particular, its size and complexity. With early contractor engagement becoming more prevalent it is increasingly likely that on public sector and large-scale projects the contractor will be responsible for this strategy, with the lead designer (also acting as the architect) being responsible on smaller, private sector projects.

Without a doubt, the main challenge from the lead designer's perspective is ensuring that those developing the Construction Strategy are limited to producing an appropriate level of definition. Considering too much detail during this stage can be disruptive to the design process and can unnecessarily divert design resources from concentrating on the development of the Concept Design.

Level of definition

Information Exchanges or deliverables are frequently framed in professional services agreements using scale. For example, 1:100 elevations or 1:5 details. In the shift from a drawing-based to a modelling-based environment, where geometry is at full size (1:1), this method no longer works. A means of defining the level of definition appropriate at each stage is needed and initiatives are under way to bring greater clarity to the geometry and data required for each aspect of a project at each stage.

What aspects might the Health and Safety Strategy consider at Stage 2?

The RIBA Plan of Work 2013 makes a shift from earlier versions by not referring to specific health and safety legislation. The Health and Safety Strategy might consider:

I health and safety legislation
I health and safety best practice
I client-specific initiatives
I industry-specific initiatives, such as the Considerate Constructors scheme (www.ccscheme.org.uk/).

The lead designer may wish to consider industry-specific health and safety initiatives in relation to the design process, such as Safety in Design. To raise the health and safety bar the lead designer might organise a number of health and safety CPD sessions at the early design team meetings, with the aim of instilling a culture of considering this important subject during the design stages.

What is a design status schedule?

A design status schedule is a useful tool for the lead designer. It performs a number of tasks:

I communicating the status of the design to the client and project lead
I allowing each design team member to understand the context of their own design work

| permitting the lead designer to convey actions required to progress coordination matters
| enabling the cost consultant to make appropriate cost allowances
| allowing assumptions or design risks to be transparent until they are closed out
| facilitating a better understanding of the design status to the contractor to allow design risks or buildability aspects to be considered, depending on the procurement process status.

The design status schedule enables the lead designer to demonstrate that the design team is being successfully led and that the coordination is progressing as planned. While meeting minutes can record formal discussions, they are not an effective way of recording and monitoring workshops, where different items are discussed on different occasions and in a less formal manner. A design status schedule can perform this task and, if properly established, this tool can be used to perform a number of functions at different stages of the project. As well as recording discussions and agreements at design workshops, it can be used to:

| record discussions associated with the development of structural engineering and mechanical services designs at the early stages of the project, such as the:
  o development of structural grids
  o progress of plant room and riser schedules
  o development of utilities
  o status of mechanical and electrical schematics
| demonstrate that the coordination of design is taking place
| tie in with Stage 2 programmes and record the status of key iterative elements of design
| discuss and record cost allowances, the level of specification or design aspects where additional cost plan allowances are required
| categorise the importance of items (hot topics)
| flag up elements where responses from utilities companies or other third parties are preventing aspects of the design from being progressed
| inform the contractor at tender stage of the status of the design and allow them to:
  o understand the status of the design and determine an appropriate level of risk in a design and build form of contract
  o take cognisance of the elements of performance specified work or contractor designed items being prepared by the team
| register all of the design risks on the project.

If a spreadsheet format is used for generating the schedule, the following headings might be considered:

I Date item raised
I Date item last discussed
I Date resolution required by
I Design lead for item
I Uniclass or CI/SfB (or other classification) reference
I Level of importance (this could be aligned with hot topics).

Items can remain on the schedule until they are satisfactorily closed out, and once this has been recorded they would be removed before the next issue. The design status schedule is 'live' document, being circulated on a regular basis. The spreadsheet format also allows sorting by consultant, date, hot topic or other headings that the lead designer might wish it to include.

An example of a design status schedule, showing what one might contain, is given in figure 2.5.

Depending on the size of the project, a number of schedules might be created for different purposes; for example, for coordination, or for conveying design information to the cost consultant.

What are hot topics?

There will always be a number of issues on any project at any given point in time, regardless of its size or sector. These can be corralled into the design status schedule – figure 2.5 contains examples of such issues. A good lead designer will define them, get on top of them as promptly as possible and manage their closure as efficiently as possible. Such issues might be called 'hot topics'. Failure to deal quickly and effectively with these issues might impact on design work, and they will not go away until they are resolved. The design status schedule assists the resolution process. On projects where this proves difficult, an additional column can be added to the schedule highlighting the number of weeks an item has been on the list. This adds to the peer pressure applied in design team meetings, encouraging the relevant parties to conclude any outstanding issues.

Example design status schedule

Date raised	Date last discussed	Raised by	Item raised	Action required and/or status	Priority	Action by (date)	Action by (who)	Status
22-Jan-14	22-Jan-14	Arch	Stone proposed for east and west elevations.	Architect to obtain samples and check costs with cost consultant prior to presenting to client. Meeting date to be tentatively agreed with planners to discuss.	1	28-Feb-14	Arch	Live
22-Jan-14	12-Feb-14	M&E	New location and size for LV (low voltage) substation to be checked.	M&E engineer to confirm that LV room position is acceptable.	1	N/A	M&E	Live
29-Jan-14	12-Feb-14	Arch	Bracing strategy for cores to be adjusted to allow full-height strip of glazing at half landings.	C&S engineer to confirm that revised bracing strategy is acceptable.	1	22-Feb-14	C&S	Live
29-Jan-14	12-Feb-14	M&E	Extent of glazing on north elevation may not comply with regulations.	Architect to review specification of glass and spandrel panels to allow M&E engineer to make an early desktop assessment on proposals.	1	28-Feb-14	Arch	Live
12-Feb-14	12-Feb-14	Fire	Design currently proposes restaurant use at the base of the atrium.	Fire engineer to confirm that proposed use will be acceptable or advise on appropriate measures. If discussions with the local authority are required an early meeting is to be arranged.	3	22-Feb-14	FE	Live
22-Feb-14	22-Feb-14	Arch	Current layout shows plantroom adjacent to the boardroom.	Acoustic engineer to advise on wall thicknesses or other strategic measures required to ensure that boardroom will have suitable environment.	2	28-Feb-14	Ac.Eng	Live

Figure 2.5   Stage 2 design status schedule

What Information Exchanges are common at Stage 2?

The previous chapter stressed the importance of agreeing the Information Exchanges for each stage during Stage 1 to allow them to be imbedded into the professional services contracts; however, discussion of what might be delivered at each stage was deferred to the relevant chapter. The Information Exchange at Stage 2 is the Concept Design, which comprises:

I outline structural and building services design
I Project Strategies
I Cost Information
I Final Project Brief.

At present, there are no guidelines on the appropriate level of definition for this Information Exchange, although, as set out in Stage 4, this will change in the future. The core considerations in defining the Information Exchange for this stage are the purposes of the information as set out below. It is also useful to consider the questions that the client may wish to have answered with this particular Information Exchange.

At Stage 2, the purpose of the information is straightforward:

I It demonstrates that the requirements set out in the Initial Project Brief are being achieved. If they are not, it explains why not.
I It summarises any changes to the Initial project Brief as incorporated into the Final Project Brief.
I It illustrates that satisfactory spatial arrangements and relationships have been developed.
I It allows the outline specification to be presented and accepted or commented on.
I It illustrates the proposed elevations and materials as presented and accepted or commented on by the client (3D images may be required to achieve this).
I It demonstrates that the proposals can be achieved with the Project Budget.
I It allows the client and the project lead to be satisfied that sufficient detail has been prepared to enable Stage 3 to be instructed.

One crucial point is that a Stage 2 report traditionally comprises a written narrative with drawings as appendices. In future, this report may comprise an executive summary with references to the Project Strategies. In a Building Information Modelling (BIM) environment, fly throughs and other dynamic presentations will become more commonplace and reports will shift to cloud environments where they can be structured differently. The lead designer is typically responsible for coordinating stage reports and so will need to be abreast of such developments, as sign-off and other management processes shift towards digital platforms that are aligned with a model-based design environment.

Plain language questions (PLQs)

A set of PLQs have been developed by the UK government's BIM Task Group to clarify thinking on this subject. The questions aim to ensure that Information Exchanges focus on answering the client's questions (as noted above), and don't just present what is important, or perceived to be important, to the design team. It is likely that this initiative will be short lived, and that once industry-wide tools that set levels of definition, Schedules of Services and design responsibilities are available, it will have served its purpose.

Chapter summary 2

Stage 2 presents significant design management challenges which the lead designer must deal with. The architect developing the Concept Design must take cognisance of the design work of the other design team members led by the lead designer, the various Project Strategies and other project information and must ensure that progress is coordinated and consistent. The iterative design process can be difficult to manage, and maintaining a light touch to allow creativity to flourish can be challenging. Designing to cost creates other design management hurdles as the cost consultant may not obtain sufficient information until the design period has been substantially completed. Managing the inputs from the client and other project stakeholders and third parties adds to the challenges involved in devising a robust and effective Design Programme.

Stage 3

Developed Design

Chapter overview

While the Stage 2 design work has the greatest impact on the design outcomes, Stage 3 must be diligently and successfully undertaken if the client's Project Outcomes are to be achieved. With the Concept Design signed off by the client at the end of Stage 2 and many of the third party issues addressed, Stage 3 is when the lead designer must lead the design team to greatest effect. The Information Exchanges at Stage 3 comprise the design information that is coordinated including any Project Strategies or other Project Information. The aim of Stage 3 is to test the Concept Design further, including through the development of specifications and Cost Information. More importantly, its aim is to ensure that the Project Outcomes are on track before the level of detail and amount of information produced are significantly increased at Stage 4.

The key coverage in this chapter is as follows:

What are the Core Objectives of Stage 3?

What procurement activities are necessary at Stage 3?

Why should the lead designer be interested in the Employer's Requirements and Contractor's Proposals?

What influences the Project Programme at Stage 3?

How does town planning influence design management at Stage 3?

What supporting tasks should be undertaken during Stage 3?

What Information Exchanges occur at Stage 3?

Introduction

The previous chapter stressed the importance of the core relationship between the architect and the client at Stage 2 and the importance of a robust Concept Design. The lead designer's input during Stage 2 is light touch, albeit strategic in nature. At Stage 3, the converse is true: the lead designer takes centre stage and plays a pivotal role, guiding the design team towards delivering a coordinated Developed Design.

In some respects the challenges presented at Stage 3 will depend on how rigorous the lead designer's strategic work has been at Stage 2. If the right coordination exercises have been undertaken and the outline building services systems and structural aspects have been carefully considered and progressed accordingly, the Developed Design stage will start from a solid platform.

Before considering what tasks occur at Stage 3, and the lead designer's contribution to these, it is essential to consider what is meant by coordination. To put it simply, at the end of Stage 3, all the information produced by the design team should be in harmony. There should be no overlapping or contradictory information. This is increasingly referred to as 'clash free' or 'clash managed' information. This subject is considered in greater detail in the Information Exchanges section at the end of the chapter.

During Stage 3 the challenge for the lead designer is to ensure that flesh is put onto the strategic bones of Stage 2 in sufficient detail to allow each member of the design team to develop their work independently at Stage 4. The two design management complexities at Stage 3 relate to third party contributors and the level of detail contained in the Project Strategies. Both of these subjects are considered in greater detail in this chapter.

At Stage 3, Change Control Procedures kick in. These are important to the lead designer as they act as a means of managing changes to the Concept Design, bearing in mind that any agreed and instructed change may result in additional design costs. Change control is considered on page 103.

One significant challenge is that there is currently no single document that sets out what the Information Exchanges at the end of the stage should be. While there are moves afoot to change this, it is a crucial topic for the lead designer and is considered in greater detail at the end of this chapter.

What are the Core Objectives of this stage?

The Core Objectives of the RIBA Plan of Work 2013 at Stage 3 are:

At Stage 3, the Stage 2 information progresses to the next level of definition and is updated in line with any coordination work. The aim is ensure that the Concept Design is robust and coordinated before the greatest amount of information is produced at Stage 4, ahead of construction.

It needs to be remembered that the Concept Design starts with the Initial Project Brief and that the Stage 2 activities take place in a short space of time and any coordination exercises are very strategic in nature. Conversely, at Stage 4, the lion's share of information is produced and the smallest of details must be resolved. Stage 3 sits between these two diverse stages: at this stage, the design team ensures that the Concept Design is robust and takes it to the next level of detail before Stage 4 commences. By the end of Stage 3 the design must be sufficiently robust and detailed for a planning consent application to be submitted to the relevant local authority.

How does coordination work impact on the Developed Design?

Increasingly shorter project timescales mean that the progression from a blank screen to a Concept Design must be rapid. This inevitably limits the coordination exercises that can realistically be undertaken at Stage 2, therefore the lead designer must select these high-level studies wisely. As set out in the previous chapter, these could include the analysis of typical structural bays, the selection of the type of frame and an estimate of the plant room and riser sizes for incorporation into the plans. The lead designer would use this information to determine aspects such as the floor-to-floor height, bearing in mind that this in turn will determine the length of stairways and influence the overall height of the building.

At Stage 3, the entire building is analysed in greater detail. So far, this guide has not mentioned the implications of working in a Building Information Modelling (BIM) environment because the creative nature of Stage 2 means that practices will use a range of design and presentation tools. While CAD will continue to be used for some time, practices of all sizes are seeing the benefits of using BIM. As BIM greatly assists the coordination process, it comes into its own at Stage 3.

BIM models contain 3D geometric information, which can be reviewed more effectively than 2D CAD information, and also hold or link to other types of data, allowing many tasks to be driven by a 'single source of truth'. Geometric tasks that a BIM model can be used for include:

I developing structural beam sizes for the whole building (which is easier once the frame type has been determined)
I testing space allocations for plant rooms and risers, to ratify their robustness
I developing building cores, including consideration of toilet and stair arrangements in greater detail
I examining in greater detail the spatial arrangements associated with the building services schematics, such as drainage, water supply, low-voltage distribution and other systems
I considering the building elevations in greater detail, including their environmental criteria (related primarily to the mechanical engineering design, cost, materials and construction methodologies).

Accepting that there is an overlap between geometric tasks and data-driven studies (eg data calculations are required to determine beam sizes), the latter might include:

I determining deflections and sizes of structural beams and columns
I calculating environmental conditions
I determining duct and pipework sizes.

In a BIM environment the core designers will develop their own 3D models, which will be brought together (federated) on a regular basis within a common data environment using collaborative processes, such as those set out in PAS1192-2:2013. The lead designer's role is to review these individual models at each iteration, and to steer the changes and developments required to them before they are uploaded for incorporation into the next version of the federated model.

This is ideally done in a proactive manner, rather than via the use of software that detects clashes (clash detection), to allow any conflicts to be discussed and resolved. Clash detection software should be used for checking purposes, rather than as a design tool per se.

Common BIM terms

PAS1192-2:2013

This is a specification that sets out the methodology for producing a federated model in a common data environment, including the structure and processes required to facilitate this.

Federated model

A federated model comprises all of the 3D BIM models of the design team. The models are reviewed by the lead designer before they are uploaded to the common data environment (CDE). The federated model includes a mix of geometric information and data. Connected files can also be uploaded to the CDE so they can be used by other parties. The federated model allows each designer to work with 'static' reference models as they produce their own design information, which allows different aspects to be progressed at the same time. The core difference between using a federated model and a 'live' model is that the time lag between each iteration of the federated model can result in inconsistencies being introduced into the individual models (which are subsequently identified as clashes). The lead designer's role is crucial in dealing with any such issues before the individual models are uploaded to the federated model.

Common BIM terms (*continued*)

Common data environment (CDE)

The CDE is where the current BIM information is saved, and where it can be referred to or utilised by any member of the project team. Typically, a third party provider manages the CDE; this allows an independent verification of what was uploaded and when, if such information is required.

Live model

Increasingly, multidisciplinary design teams work in a BIM environment that uses 'live' design information, avoiding the need for regular uploading and federation of their design information to a CDE. This way of working requires innovative and new design methods, and a robust Design Programme is needed to define the timing of each designer's contribution. The lead designer has to have a good understanding of who will be designing what for this method to be successful.

One major change in a BIM environment is that each design profession typically runs a number of software packages during the development of their 3D geometric models. In addition, the cost consultant is able to derive quantities from the federated model using model-based cost estimating software, allowing faster and more iterative cost reviews of the developing design.

While all of these processes speed up the lead designer's ability to review the design proposals as they progress, it needs to be remembered that the lead designer should always be proactively considering how the different designs will come together, with a view to achieving 'clash free' integration. Put another way, in a BIM environment the processes used to ensure the design is properly coordinated are fundamentally no different, but the review processes are faster, more robust and more transparent.

What changes to the outline proposals might take place at Stage 3?

The development of the outline proposals at Stage 3 is a crucial subject to consider. Fundamentally, the outline proposals developed at Stage 2 should be developed further, but the Concept Design itself should not be revisited unless the development work necessities this. To consider this idea requires an understanding of the difference between a change to the Concept Design and its design development. This is certainly a topic that the lead designer should be aware of and is covered in detail in the section on change control on page 103.

The simple logic is that if the client has signed off the Concept Design then none of the spatial aspects of the building should change during Stage 3. The elevations work to the same principles but have different drivers. It is likely that more detailed studies will be undertaken during Stage 3, requiring changes to the Stage 2 proposals. This presents fewer issues as such studies would not typically impede the development of the plans, and cost checks would confirm that the developing proposals are still affordable. However, in a BIM environment, the work of the other designers is more sensitive to such changes. For example:

| changing from lightweight aluminium panels to stonework will change the required depths of the perimeter edge beams
| a higher percentage of glazing will increase heat loads in the spaces behind, requiring increased duct sizes and possibly impacting on the environmental credentials of the building.

This greater sensitivity underlines the efficiencies of BIM technologies, but it also demonstrates the different challenges faced by the lead designer in this environment. The challenges in a 3D environment, where geometry and data are interlinked, are fundamentally different from those created in a 2D CAD environment, where information needs to be coordinated but exists in independent 'silos'.

The challenge for the lead designer is not in understanding how the various BIM technologies work, but in understanding how they might alter or dictate the timing of design contributions by each design team member differently to CAD processes and how these contributions might be more effectively carried out. For example, there is no point in the M&E engineer running software calculations to determine if the environmental criteria set in the brief are being met in each space if the architect is on the verge of uploading a model that has a different external wall.

In summary, the Concept Design is developed in a way that ensures the Developed Design is robust. The lead designer needs to focus not just on the resolution of geometric aspects of the design, but also on how this information will inform the data produced and, more crucially, how the geometric model may impact on the various software packages used by the engineers to analyse the building and produce their layouts.

Why is the outline specification reviewed at Stage 3?

The outline specification is closely linked to the Cost Information produced at Stage 2 and substantial changes are unlikely to be required during Stage 3. Changes may be required to fine-tune the design as it is coordinated or in response to the Stage 3 Cost Information as it develops. Stage 4 deals with the next substantive level of specification development.

Stage 3 is focused more on the geometric aspects of the project and the development of the Project Strategies, rather than on the development of the specification per se. That said, Stage 3 may allow time for product specifications to be considered further and for the presentation and agreement of specific products with the client. The journey from descriptive to prescriptive through Stage 2 to Stage 4 will be unique to each project and each client and dependent on the Information Exchanges agreed at Stage 1. A simple rule is that Stage 3 should be focused on the specification of 'what you can see' and on the aspects of the design that may impact on design Quality Objectives.

What might impact on Cost Information at Stage 3?

The crucial difference between Stages 2 and 3 from a cost perspective is that Stage 3 commences with a Concept Design. This sets the scene for the cost consultant because detailed cost exercises can be undertaken from the start of the stage. Therefore, a core activity at the start of Stage 3 is for the lead designer to sit down with the cost consultant and agree what aspects of the design need to be considered in greater detail or where additional information is required in order to increase the granularity of the cost plan and reduce the contingencies that have been incorporated into it. Exercises undertaken might include reviews of the following:

❘ The assumptions made by the cost consultant.
It is inevitable that the level of detail required at Stage 2, be it geometric or data (such as the specification), will mean that assumptions have been made at Stage 2. At Stage 3, an important first task is to review those assumptions, allowing adjustments to be made accordingly. For example, has the cost consultant assumed the subfloor will be constructed in timber, screed or a raised floor system?

| The detail of the specification

Stage 2 specifications, if produced, may not contain sufficient detail to allow adequate cost allowances to be made. For example, a one-hour fire-rated timber veneered door with vision panels and stainless steel ironmongery will be more expensive than an unrated painted timber door with nylon ironmongery. Early discussions on such detail are essential to allow them to be addressed in the cost estimate as early as possible during Stage 3. Some clients and/or practices may have taken a view on such items at Stage 2, but it is possible that the granularity of the cost plan does not allow this level of detail to be absorbed and so a high level of contingency is likely to be allocated regardless of the increased level of detail.

| The cost of detail

During Stage 3 the architect will consider in greater detail the head, jamb and cill details on the project. Clearly, a 300 mm aluminium trim around a window will be more expensive than a flush window detail. Indeed, even a two-brick return may have cost implications, depending on the cost allowances and assumptions made at Stage 2. The key here is to ensure that sufficient exercises are undertaken without driving too far into Stage 4 information. This is a core Information Exchange issue.

| The impact of Research and Development

It is possible that a new or innovative cladding system or approach is proposed. Early cost discussions with specialist subcontractors will be required to provide accurate estimates. These exercises are typically called 'market testing', which simply means determining the cost of something for which there is no historical benchmark information. These discussions will need to continue and become more focused during Stage 3.

In summary, cost exercises led by the lead designer at Stage 3 should help eliminate assumptions made at Stage 2, clarify the specification for all aspects of the design and allow a review of the contingency allowances. Some clients or design teams may have worked together on previous projects, allowing a greater degree of fine-tuning at Stage 2. Either approach is acceptable as long as the lead designer ensures that appropriate contingency allowances are included in the cost plan.

What influences the Project Strategies at Stage 3?

In a similar vein to the rest of the design, the level of detail in the Project Strategies will increase during Stage 3. The lead designer needs to be mindful of this increased level of detail and must review all Project Strategies to ratify that they are complementary and do not contradict each other, as well as ensuring that they are aligned with the geometric information in the PIM.

Certain strategies may not have been essential to the Stage 2 design and will be developed from scratch during Stage 3. Some strategies will have connected and related themes. The Project Strategies are therefore crucial tools to be harnessed by the lead designer during Stage 3. They:

I can be used to explain detailed operational or In Use aspects to the client
I help to test the robustness of the Stage 2 design
I allow individual design team members to explain detailed aspects of their work
I enable high-level strategies, developed during Stage 2, to be developed to the next level of detail
I allow specialists to contribute their advice in a project-focused manner.

The strategies of importance to a client, as they may influence working methods or operational aspects in use, need particular attention early on in the stage. A good starting point at the beginning of the stage is to determine what Project Strategies need to be reviewed and signed off by the client, and also to consider which will require information from other members of the design team before they can be commenced and which may relate to each other in some way or have connected themes. It may be beneficial to include timelines for such strategies in the Design Programme.

Some Project Strategies may be of little interest to the client but may be crucial to the development of the design. Some will not progress beyond Stage 3, as they contain sufficient detail to allow another designer to develop their aspect of the design during Stage 4. With this diversity, the lead designer must be aware of the purpose of each Project Strategy, know who will produce and contribute to each one, and ensure that they are all sufficiently robust for their intended purpose. Project Strategies at Stage 3 might include the following:

| Acoustic strategy

The acoustic strategy is typically produced by an acoustician to address noise issues related to the site or acoustically sensitive areas within a building. For example:

o   noise from a motorway or railway
o   noise between a retail unit (pub) on the ground floor and residences above
o   noise between classrooms in a school or university
o   specialist areas, such as recording studios.

A report will be produced that identifies areas that need acoustic attenuation or other treatment, guided by the Initial Project Brief, British Standards or sector-specific or other guidance. It may also cover possible specification requirements, such as the specification for windows. The acoustic strategy will largely be technical in its nature, but the client may also be interested in its contents.

| Fire engineering strategy

The Stage 2 fire engineering strategy will have addressed the core issues, such as the details around an atrium, which may have been crucial to the Concept Design development. At Stage 3 the strategy will consider these concepts in greater detail. For example:

o   the area of smoke vents required and where these are located
o   the types of screens to be used around the atrium and their fire rating
o   the need for sprinklers or other mitigation items that may have cost implications.

Consultation with local fire or building control authorities may also have been carried out to determine if the design is acceptable in principle, with the detail followed up and agreed during Stage 3.

| Security strategy

The security strategy is a good example of a short-term strategy that assists the design team by clearly presenting to the client what is proposed. It will identify:

o   perimeter fencing and entrance provisions
o   alarm contacts on windows and doors
o   CCTV provision
o   external lighting and other such measures.

This and similar Project Strategies are an excellent means of clearly explaining what is being provided in relation to a single design aspect, allowing the client to comment on its suitability and for the cost estimate to be fine-tuned accordingly. Sometimes such Project Strategies will flag up overprovision, and at other times the client may request additional measures. Either way, they underpin any discussions and agreements, allowing Stage 4 information to be prepared with the confidence that the design meets the client's requirements.

In summary, Project Strategies are produced for many reasons. Most importantly, they effectively communicate to the client the rationale behind any decision making. Most importantly, they allow Developed Design information to be prepared with greater confidence and less likelihood of change.

From the lead designer's perspective, the Project Strategies assist client sign-off and benefit the coordination of all aspects of the building. They are therefore a crucial asset in the design management process.

What drives the Design Programme during Stage 3?

With the Concept Design signed off by the client, the emphasis shifts from the architect's work and liaison with the client and a light touch from the other design team members to substantial work between design team members to produce the coordinated design at the end of Stage 3. As well as the design team, other stakeholders, such as the planners, need to be consulted in greater detail.

This shift in emphasis is underlined in the Stage 3 Design Programme set out in figure 3.1. More activities are focused on cost, specification and coordination exercises. While less input is required from the client, regular meetings with the client are scheduled in order to address any hot topics or issues arising from consultations or design development.

The core emphasis continues to be to use the Design Programme in conjunction with other design tools, such as the design status schedule, to record and disseminate design decisions to the project team. The Design Programme should also set out, where possible, any key consultations and discussions with third parties that may impact on the development of the design.

Is a design status schedule useful during Stage 3?

The design status schedule can be used in a similar manner as in Stage 2, to assist the lead designer in conveying the status of the design

Stage 3 Design Programme

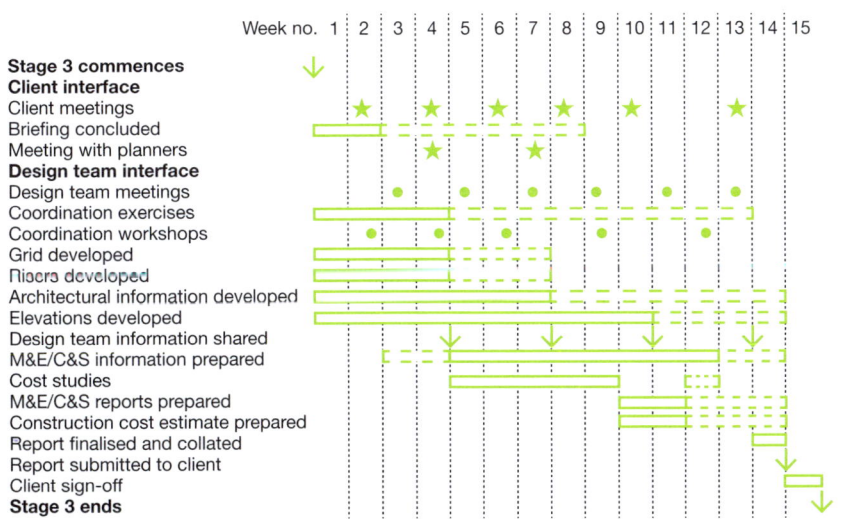

Figure 3.1   Stage 3 Design Programme

and to highlight the aspects that each design team member should be focusing on. Hot topics will arise throughout the design process and so the schedule will continue to assist with driving any such issues swiftly to conclusion.

What procurement activities are necessary at Stage 3?

During Stage 3, the choice of procurement route will not fundamentally affect the design activities of the design team, but the contributions of other project team members will vary depending on the procurement route selected.

On a traditional project the design team will prepare its designs without the contractor's input, although a specialist construction adviser may undertake the construction lead role or advise on buildability or other construction-related matters.

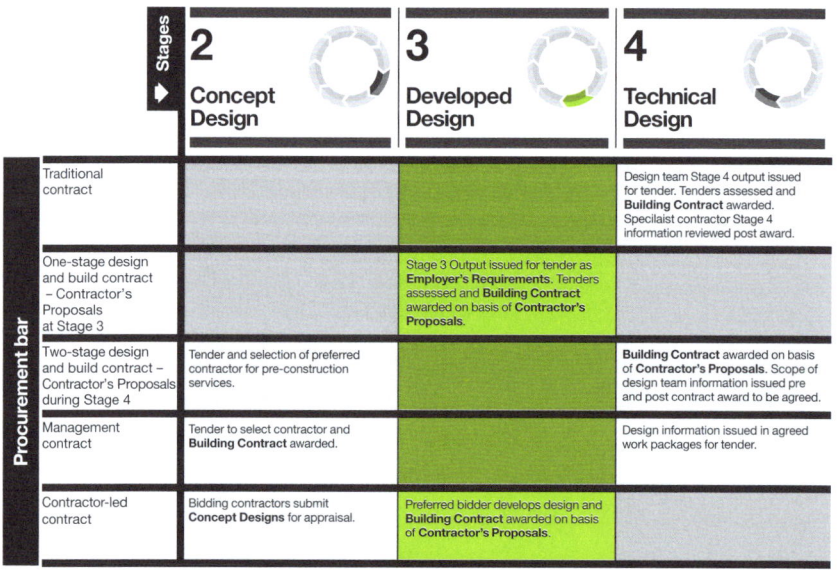

Figure 3.2   Procurement activities during Stages 2 to 4 for different procurement routes (Stage 3 highlighted)

On a two-stage design and build project, the contractor will be part of the project team and will advise the design team as the Developed Design progresses. Similarly, on a management contract the tendering of packages will be under way, particularly for the enabling and front-end structural packages, and it is possible that Stage 5 will have already commenced.

Figure 3.2 highlights that core procurement activities will be taking place during Stage 3 on the one-stage design and build and contractor-led procurement routes. A crucial consideration is that although the Stage 3 Information Exchanges could theoretically be the same for these routes, their purposes are fundamentally different. On a single-stage design and build project, they would form part of the Employer's Requirements issued for tender, whereas on a contractor-led project they would form part of the Contractor's Proposals included within the Building Contract. From the lead designer's perspective, this is a good time to consider the difference between these two core sets of project documentation.

What are the Employer's Requirements?

The Employer's Requirements (ERs) form the backbone of a design and build tender invitation, which will ask the contractor to accept design responsibility. The contents of ERs will vary depending on the stage at which they are issued. As each design stage progresses, the design becomes more fixed and the contractor will be less able to influence it. Forms of procurement that include detailed and prescriptive requirements are typically nicknamed 'design and dump' – the client has all but completed the design that they want and is simply transferring risk to the contractor.

The ERs will contain a mixture of prescriptive and descriptive items, and different elements of the design will be at different levels of detail. The percentages of prescriptive and descriptive items can vary regardless of the level of definition. The specification is a core vehicle for fine-tuning these percentages. For example:

I Performance criteria may be given for certain elements, allowing the contractor to use their supply chain to complete the design and giving them a degree of latitude to innovate. These aspects would typically be included as Contractor's Designed Portions in a traditional project. Examples would include the curtain walling or handrail designs.
I Certain elements may be defined in a descriptive manner in the specification using British Standards or their equivalents, allowing the contractor to determine suppliers and products. Such products might include wall tiles, blockwork and other aspects that will be concealed in the final works.
I Certain elements may be defined in a descriptive manner, with 'representative' but not mandated products included in the specification, allowing the contractor to determine suppliers and products, albeit subject to samples being submitted and approved by the client. Such products might include visible elements on the project, such as toilet fittings, doors and ironmongery, ceiling and floor finishes.
I Some items may be prescriptive in their nature, allowing the contractor no leeway to change them. This might include the smallest of components; for example, a retail client might use a particular external lock on all of their projects or a hotel chain might require particular sanitaryware to be used.

Table 3.1 illustrates how the information included in ERs varies depending on the procurement route.

Table 3.1   Employer's Requirements contents

PROCUREMENT ROUTE	BRIEF	DESIGN INFORMATION
One-stage design and build	Final Project Brief	Stage 3 Information Exchange
Two-stage design and build	Initial Project Brief	None or partial Stage 2 information
Contractor-led procurement	Initial Project Brief	None

The brief also services a core purpose within the ERs, particularly where a Concept or Developed Design has not been incorporated. The brief can become a core contractual requirement, against which the Contractor's Proposals are checked. Furthermore, the Contractor's Proposals are unlikely to address every aspect of the brief and the Final Project Brief therefore needs to make sure that it properly sets out the expected criteria for any residual aspects of the design. As set out in earlier chapters, this contractual requirement requires the brief to be considered in greater detail at Stage 1 and also at Stage 2.

Figure 2.1 outlines the descriptive to prescriptive journey. The ERs commence the contractual part of the journey, and although the general rule is that the more stage design work that is undertaken, the more prescriptive the ERs will be (particularly in relation to the building's form and appearance), the specification can allow a degree of latitude for the contractor so they can harness their supply chain to greatest effect.

What are the Contractor's Proposals?

The Contractor's Proposals (CPs) are the contractor's formal response to the ERs. Stage information is typically used, as set out in table 3.2.

In some instances (one-stage design and build) the CPs might comprise a mark-up of the ERs or the contractor might confirm that the ERs are acceptable in their entirety. On a contractor-led project they will comprise a comprehensive set of Stage 2 or 3 information. On a two-stage design

Table 3.2   Contractor's Proposals

PROCUREMENT ROUTE	DESIGN INFORMATION
One-stage design and build	Stage 3 Information Exchange
Two-stage design and build	Partial Stage 4 information
Contractor-led procurement	Stage 2 or 3 Information Exchange

and build project they may comprise a mix of design team and specialist subcontractor information. There are a number of crucial considerations:

How are elements that are not designed to be dealt with?

As the CPs will not comprise the completed Stage 4 information, a methodology needs to be agreed for how the contractor is to complete the design in accordance with any residual briefing items contained within the ERs included in the Building Contract. In some instances, information will need to be completed and signed off by the Employer's Agent. Once the Building Contract has been concluded, the contractor needs a degree of flexibility to complete the design. The boundaries of this flexibility therefore need to be clear.

Why should the lead designer be interested in the ERs and CPs?

The lead designer should be extremely interested in the contents of the ERs and the CPs because:

I the level of design included can vary substantially between the two. For example, on a two-stage design and build project, the ERs may comprise the Stage 2 Information Exchanges with the CPs containing Stage 4 information from the design team and the specialist subcontractors
I both sets of documents will contain design work that has not been completed and may not be coordinated
I even where the CPs are incorporated into the Building Contract, the contractor may still have contractual obligations to comply with certain aspects of the ERs.

In simple terms, the issue from the lead designer's perspective is not what has been included in the two sets of documents but what is not included, as this incomplete or uncoordinated design work will need to be allowed for in the contractor's tender/contract sum. Even where there is such an allowance, such work represents a risk to the contractor until they are able to pass the risk on to their subcontractors. Clearly, the earlier the ERs are produced, the less developed the design information will be.

Where Stage 2 or 3 Information Exchanges are incorporated into the ERs, a design status schedule is a useful tool for the lead designer to use to convey the status of each aspect of the design as part of the tender documentation. Tracking the status of each aspect of the design allows the contractor to price future design development and risk accordingly. CAD or BIM information can easily convey the impression that it is further developed than it actually is – the design status schedule allows the lead designer to correct any such assumptions.

While the majority of the risks on a design and build project are those linked to incomplete design work, and the associated coordination, or issues encountered on site, perhaps due to buildability or sequencing problems or a delay by a subcontractor, the contractor may also accept further risks, such as the risks associated with discharging certain planning conditions attached to the planning consent or concluding discussions with utilities companies. While the contractor will have accepted the inclusion of such risks in the Building Contract, the lead designer can assist in risk mitigation by framing the risks properly in the first instance and then ensuring that any design risks are managed until they are closed out.

Why is design development a crucial consideration on design and build projects?

As highlighted above, the ERs and the CPs are inevitably based on an incomplete design. Where a design is incomplete, there can be a fine line between completing the design (design development) and changing the design, which would, strictly speaking, require the use of Change Control Procedures.

What influences the Project Programme at Stage 3?

If the Concept Design is robust and the Project Programme incorporates a reasonable period for accommodating the Stage 3 Design Programme, there is no reason why the Project Programme should alter at this stage. That said, Change Control Procedures commence during this stage and a major change to the design could delay the design period. It is therefore prudent to have a programme contingency in the Project Programme to accommodate any project risks that might create delay, particularly those created by third parties outside the direct control of the design team. For example, when the Concept Design is presented in detail to the local authority planners for the first time, there is a risk that the planners may require adjustments that impact on the coordination exercises being carried out.

How does town planning influence design management at Stage 3?

The planning application is typically submitted at the end of Stage 3. The amount of information to be produced has increased over the years – this is considered in the Information Exchanges section below.

As the preparation of this information is likely to occur in parallel with other Stage 3 activities, the lead designer's main role is to ensure that, as the supporting information is produced, it is robust and does not contradict any of the Project Strategies or other information being developed. The planning process is covered in greater detail in *RIBA Plan of Work 2013 Guide: Town Planning.*

What supporting tasks should be undertaken during Stage 3?

The Suggested Key Support Tasks at Stage 3 comprise the following:

| Review and update Sustainability, Maintenance and Operational and Handover Strategies and Risk Assessments.
| Undertake third party consultations as required and conclude Research and Development aspects.
| Review and update Project Execution Plan, including Change Control Procedures.
| Review and update Construction and Health and Safety Strategies.

At Stage 3 the majority of supporting tasks involve the updating of Project Strategies produced during Stage 3. Many of the strategies outlined above will be completed at the end of Stage 3; however, the core Project Strategies in the Suggested Key Support Tasks task bar will continue to evolve during Stage 4 and beyond. Their contents are considered below.

How might the Sustainability Strategy change at Stage 3?

The main purpose of the Sustainability Strategy at Stage 3 is to ensure that the Developed Design continues to reflect and underpin the client's Sustainability Aspirations. The main emphasis at Stage 3 would be to:

I ensure that any formal sustainability assessments are progressing as planned
I consider any Building Regulations aspects (such as the Part L assessment or design stage carbon/energy declaration) that may require consultation with the relevant authorities
I review the design and identify opportunities within the Construction Strategy.

A number of parties within the project team may be responsible for developing the Sustainability Strategy and ensuring that the checkpoints are achieved. The challenge from the lead designer's perspective is ensuring that the work of the design team reflects the contents of the Sustainability Strategy. Opportunities to discuss this can usefully be included early in the Design Programme. It is essential that the Sustainability Strategy is developed holistically, and not in isolation, if the Developed Design is to be coordinated at the end of the stage.

What influences the Maintenance and Operational Strategy at Stage 3?

The Stage 3 Maintenance and Operational Strategy builds on the detail established at Stage 2. For example, it may have been deemed that the most appropriate method of cleaning the windows of a four-storey further education college is to use a cherry picker. It may also have been agreed that the provision of a cherry picker sits outside the capital expenditure budget (ie it is not included in the construction cost estimate) and a location for storing it may have been identified. At Stage 3:

I the specification of the cherry picker might be considered further: eg reach, power supply requirements
I access around the building will be considered in greater detail: eg path widths, sub-base loadings and design
I detailed requirements will remain to be considered further: eg power supplies (dependent on specification), water points, access to the main entrance (only outside term time and at weekends?).

This simple example also underlines that the Maintenance and Operational Strategy is not solely about Stage 7: In Use activities. It is about ensuring that the aspects of the Stage 2 strategy are robust when interrogated at the next level of design detail. In terms of the M&E design, similar discussions might take place in relation to replacing the filters of an air-handling unit.

Will this be done by lift or by stair? How big are the filters? How big is the lift? In summary, Stage 3 tests the strategy developed at Stage 2. If this is not robust, alternatives can be put to, and agreed with, the client before more design work has been carried out at Stage 4. These examples also underline that this particular strategy is a crucial tool of the lead designer for developing a design that will be effective at Stage 7.

How might the Handover Strategy change at Stage 3?

Stage 3 does not include any tasks that would unduly influence the Handover Strategy; however, it is prudent to review the contents of the strategy to determine if any changes are required.

What influences the Risk Assessments during the Stage 3?

Coordination exercises will substantially reduce design risks during Stage 4 and the lead designer's design status schedule can be adjusted accordingly. It is likely that the biggest risks to be included in the project lead's Risk Assessments during Stage 3 will relate to third parties – the consultations covered in the following section will help to reduce such risks before the majority of the design work is undertaken during Stage 4.

Design risks at this stage might relate to items such as the cost of a bespoke cladding system or bespoke products or any aspect of the design that requires Research and Development. The risks imposed by these design aspects can be reduced by engaging with the specialist subcontractors or suppliers who may supply and/or construct the elements. This work can reduce the risks by informing the design process as well as providing cost and buildability advice.

Where the procurement strategy involves the transfer of risk to the contractor at the end of the stage, the lead designer will need to pay particular attention to design risks during this stage and ensure that their status is properly conveyed.

What third party consultations may be necessary at Stage 3?

Where possible, third party consultations should commence at Stage 2. For items such as road access or utilities connections, this should be straightforward. Other consultations require more developed and detailed design information and may be of limited value if they are undertaken too early. Conversely, consultations carried out too late can result in disruption to the design process. The lead designer needs to consider these points and arrange for any consultations to be undertaken and closed out as early as possible. Consultations at Stage 3 might include:

I Secure by Design
I local licensing authorities for bars and restaurants.

The lead designer may have held meetings at Stage 2 to determine likely issues or to agree the content and timing of further discussions and/or submissions. Scheduled meetings can be incorporated into the Stage 3 Design Programme. The lead designer can use the Risk Assessments and/or the design status schedule to track the status of third party consultations. This is a particularly important task because the project may be a lower priority to a third party – it is likely that unless that party is continually monitored and chased, no progress will be made, and a low risk will slowly be converted into a significant one.

One final and fairly obvious point is that the importance of any consultations will be determined by the likely impacts of any changes the third party may require. For example, changes to a road layout required by the highway authority may be ring-fenced to the work of the civil engineer, whereas changes to the elevations dictated by the planners will require updated elevations from the architect and new client consent, and may impact on cost and, possibly, on the building services design (if the percentage of glazing were to be increased, for example).

Why does Research and Development conclude at Stage 3?

Research and Development (R&D) needs to be concluded at Stage 3 to ensure that the Technical Design aspects are progressed sufficiently to allow tendering activities to be completed and that the design team and/or the specialist subcontractors can conclude the Technical Design during Stage 4. Research can also impact other matters. For example, continuing the three examples given in the previous chapter (see page 70):

I The cladding system will need to be sufficiently developed and the scope identified to allow the contractor to seek tenders from specialist subcontractors. While the timing of this will depend on the procurement route, the lead designer will want to see the specialist subcontractor appointed in sufficient time to allow the integration of their proposals into the design.

I The architect will need to be confident that the new cladding material has been suitably tested to comply with the performance criteria that will be put into the specification. Using a performance specification to specify a product that is unlikely to comply with the requirements may pass responsibility to the contractor, but it merely delays dealing with the issue until the next stage, when the contractor will come to the same conclusions and suggest different materials.

I Research may have indicated that the use of colour will improve recovery times in a hospital but not concluded which colours give the best result. The walls to be painted can be identified to allow the scope and cost to be identified, with the final selection of colours to be made at Stage 4.

In summary, R&D needs to be concluded to allow the Technical Design and tendering processes to be properly undertaken before construction commences on site at Stage 5.

Why are Change Control Procedures essential at Stage 3?

At the end of Stage 2 the Concept Design and its corresponding Information Exchanges are aligned with the Final Project Brief. During Stage 3 the amount of information produced by the design team increases and so changes can be disruptive and may incur additional design costs. It is therefore essential that any changes are properly considered, via Change Control Procedures, and signed off by the client before they are implemented. A change control form used as part of these procedures might contain:

I details of the proposed change
I the reason for the proposed change
I any design costs associated with implementing the change
I the impact on the construction cost estimate (up or down)
I the date the change was implemented.

There are two complexities in dealing with changes at Stage 3:

I Time is of the essence
  Any procedure needs to be specific in relation to timescales. Before any change is instructed, it needs to be remembered that the design

team will continue to develop the current design until instructed to do otherwise, and that if instructions are delayed further, additional design costs may be incurred.

| The design is still being developed

During Stage 3 the design is developed as it is coordinated. Coordination activity inevitably requires adjustments and refinement of the design; otherwise, the Information Exchanges at Stage 3 would be the same as at Stage 2. While there are grey areas in relation to what constitutes design *development* and what is a design *change*, a simple rule is: moving rooms or spaces around or increasing their size is a change. Adjusting a room to accommodate the development of a riser is design *development*. Moving a room in response to a client request is design *change*. This flags up the conundrum of co-ordination: it may necessitate changing the Concept Design and the spatial arrangements, which will require the agreement of the client. If strategic coordination exercises have been undertaken during Stage 2, the possibilities of this occurring are minimised.

What should the Construction Strategy consider at Stage 3?

At Stage 2 the Concept Design needs to consider and incorporate the core strategic coordination aspects, including matters such as the structural frame or any core buildability concerns. The Construction Strategy should not require any major changes during Stage 3, although it should be reviewed to consider whether any aspect of the Developed Design conflicts with the assumptions made at Stage 2. If the contractor is part of the project team during this stage it may be possible to progress aspects of the strategy in advance of the detailed design development at Stage 4.

What aspects might the Health and Safety Strategy consider at Stage 3?

At Stage 3 the lead designer will lead the development of the Health and Safety Strategy, which will be closely related to the Construction Strategy. The lead designer should work to close out any risks that were identified during Stage 2 and continue to review risks as the design is developed further. The *Guide to the RIBA Plan of Work 2013: Health and Safety* considers the Stage 3 risks in greater detail.

What Information Exchanges occur at Stage 3?

The Information Exchange at Stage 3 is the Developed Design, including:

I coordinated architectural, structural and building services design
I Project Strategies
I Cost Information.

The operative word in the Stage 3 Information Exchange is 'coordinated' and this chapter has focused on the tasks revolving around this subject. The precise definition of what a Stage 3 Information Exchange might comprise is difficult (the reasons are set out in Stage 4). Strategically, and

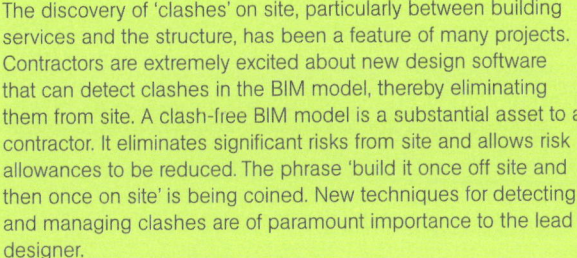

Clash detection and management

The discovery of 'clashes' on site, particularly between building services and the structure, has been a feature of many projects. Contractors are extremely excited about new design software that can detect clashes in the BIM model, thereby eliminating them from site. A clash-free BIM model is a substantial asset to a contractor. It eliminates significant risks from site and allows risk allowances to be reduced. The phrase 'build it once off site and then once on site' is being coined. New techniques for detecting and managing clashes are of paramount importance to the lead designer.

Many clashes arise from the integration of specialist subcontractors' design work at Stage 4. For example, a duct clashing with the haunch of a beam. Using traditional coordination processes the lead designer could not have identified these clashes during Stage 3, but they can now be identified when the BIM models of the specialist subcontractors are integrated into the federated model during Stage 4.

Clash detection software can be a useful quality assurance tool during Stage 3. However, this powerful tool should not be used as a design tool. The lead designer should be encouraging the use of workshops or other exercises to facilitate design coordination, so preventing any clashes in the first instance. In some instances a clash-managed BIM model may be agreed rather than a clash-free one. For example, a raised floor may have hundreds of 'clashes' with floor boxes. In this instance, the reason for the clashes is clear and resolving them serves no real purpose.

in a BIM environment, the Stage 3 Information Exchange might comprise the coordinated BIM models of the design team and Cost Information that has been derived from and is linked to the same information. The lead designer would direct the development of the federated model to an adequate level of detail to allow it to undergo a clash detection review. The Stage 3 Information Exchange would be this clash-free or clash-managed model. Of course, one issue is that such checks can only review the information contained in the models, so a final role of the lead designer is to ensure that this information has been produced by each designer.

The information developed for the Stage 3 Information Exchange will also typically be used as part of the Planning Application. Such applications include supporting documents such as an access strategy. It is important that these documents are developed in parallel with the other Project Strategies to ensure that they are coordinated with the rest of the design proposals.

Chapter summary 3

Stage 3 is an important project stage. The Information Exchanges demonstrate that the Concept Design is robust, and any substantive design issues that were residual from Stage 2 should have been ironed out at this stage, before the Technical Design is prepared at Stage 4. A core outcome of Stage 3 is that the design work is coordinated. A coordinated Stage 3 output allows Stage 4 activity, whether by a member of the design team or by a specialist subcontractor, to be undertaken more efficiently and effectively and, more crucially, with a greater degree of independence. The Stage 3 outputs should also be robust enough for a planning application to be made.

Technical Design

Chapter overview

Stage 4 is when the majority of design work is undertaken, although the nature of the design activity is entirely different from that in the earlier stages. At this stage, the focus is on the nitty-gritty detail required to construct the building at Stage 5. Stage 4 includes the design work of the design team as well as the design work of the specialist subcontractors, although the timing of such work will depend on how the procurement strategy influences the Project Programme and, in turn, the Stage 4 Design Programme.

The key coverage in this chapter is as follows:

What are the Core Objectives of Stage 4?

What procurement activities are necessary at Stage 4?

What influences the Project Programme at Stage 4?

How does town planning influence Stage 4 design management?

What supporting tasks should be undertaken during Stage 4?

What Information Exchanges occur at Stage 4?

Introduction

If Stage 4 is to be successful, it is crucial that the lead designer's contributions at Stage 3 have resulted in information that is robust enough to allow each design team member to substantially commence the preparation of their own Stage 4 Information Exchanges information independently. For example, the lift shafts should have been developed during Stage 3 to a level of detail that allows the following activities to be undertaken concurrently at Stage 4:

preparation of structural information by the structural engineer, including detailed calculations and detailed information for items such as sumps and lifting beams

development of more detailed information for the lift requirements by the M&E engineer, including the specification

drafting of the partition details by the architect, including opening sizes, fire ratings, finishes, acoustics and other criteria.

This level of independence does not mean that the work of the lead designer is complete. In fact, the lead designer continues to play a crucial role during Stage 4, as the next layer of detail is added to each party's information, requiring more detailed and granular coordination. The lead designer will contribute to each strand of the Technical Design work; for example, the lead designer will ensure that the architect liaises with the building services engineer in relation to the lift car finishes, and will facilitate any three-way conversations that may be required with the civil and structural (C&S) engineer to ensure that the lift shaft complies with the appropriate health and safety legislation.

During Stage 4 the work of the specialist subcontractors with design responsibilities is also undertaken. The lead designer will typically be responsible for ensuring that this design work is integrated into the coordinated design. The subtle difference between *coordinating* and *integrating* is that if the coordinated design has been properly considered it should remain unaltered as each specialist subcontractor develops their own aspect of the design and this work is integrated into the coordinated design. As the example below illustrates, in certain situations the process of integration may require sections of the coordinated design to be reconsidered. Change Control Procedures will be appropriate in such situations to make sure that the impact of the change is fully considered. These situations should, however, be rare and the exception to the rule. However, this example does demonstrate the level of detail that the lead designer needs to be focused on.

Example of coordination versus integration

A good example would be where the specialist subcontractor designing the curtain walling needs to increase the size of a mullion (perhaps because the space is double height and the brickwork is angled), and to accommodate this the adjacent brickwork would have to be moved slightly.

In this scenario, the lead designer and the architect agreed that the mullion centres could not be changed, in order to maintain standard glass sizes, and that it would be acceptable to move the brickwork by half a brick.

One of the major complexities of Stage 4 is that the timing of the design team's work and the design work of the specialist subcontractors can vary considerably. This is considered in greater detail in the section on procurement (see page 118).

What are the Core Objectives of this stage?

The Core Objectives of the RIBA Plan of Work 2013 at Stage 4 are:

Tasks ⬇	
Core Objectives	Prepare **Technical Design** in accordance with **Design Responsibility Matrix** and **Project Strategies** to include all architectural, structural and building services information, specialist subcontractor design and specifications, in accordance with **Design Programme**.

Although the Design Responsibility Matrix is created during Stage 1, it becomes a crucial tool during Stage 4 as the level of detail produced increases significantly and the number of designers working on the project increases due to the introduction of specialist subcontractors with design responsibility. The Design Programme therefore becomes a crucial tool for the lead designer at Stage 4, helping to ensure that information is progressed at the right time. Another important consideration is the status of many of the Project Strategies. All of these subjects are considered in greater detail below.

Why is the Design Responsibility Matrix important at Stage 4?

The Design Responsibility Matrix is generated at Stage 1 for incorporation into the various contracts. The previous two chapters have considered reasons for 'tweaking' this tool during Stages 2 and 3. At Stage 4, it becomes an essential tool and its robustness is put to the test. At this stage a large number of parties could be contributing to the design process, so if the Design Responsibility Matrix has any 'cracks', design effort could be duplicated or essential aspects of design work might not be completed. The lead designer therefore needs to be confident that the Design Responsibility Matrix contains sufficient detail to allow each designer to work unimpeded.

Where the design baton is to be handed over from a design team member to a specialist subcontractor, lack of clarity in the Design Responsibility Matrix can result in the design team member producing either too much or the wrong type of information for the specialist subcontractor. The former may not give the specialist subcontractor sufficient leeway to use their own design skills. The latter creates inefficiencies in the process and may result in the specialist subcontractor not having the right information to progress their design.

Although a greater degree of independent working is essential during this stage, certain aspects require collaborative effort and for such aspects the Design Responsibility Matrix needs to be clear. Examples include:

│ ceiling layouts, where different ceiling types will need to be coordinated with different lighting systems and a plethora of other items, such as smoke detectors, sprinkler heads and fire alarm sounders
│ floor layouts, where floor box layouts may be required in order to develop circuit and cabling diagrams as well as trunking layouts
│ subfloor arrangements, where different arrangements may have structural or building services implications and also require different methodologies for routing services (a raised floor system v screed)
│ internal blockwork walls, which may involve developing requirements for secondary support steelwork and other structural requirements, such as bed joint reinforcement.

For such items the notes contained in the Design Responsibility Matrix need to clarify design responsibility as well as which party is to produce the information that needs to be exchanged. This is illustrated in figure 4.1. If the Design Responsibility Matrix is properly assembled and aligned with the Design Programme, with design workshops helping to ensure that more complex design aspects progress efficiently, the result should be well-coordinated and integrated information.

A completed Stage 4 Design Responsibility Matrix

Element	Design responsibility	Design team		Specialist subcontractor
		Level of detail	Level of information	Level of detail
Substructure	C&S engineer	5	5	N/A
Frame/upper slabs - steel	C&S engineer	4	4	4
Fire protection	Architect	5	5	N/A
Stairs (precast)	C&S engineer	4	4	4
Brickwork/blockwork	Architect	5	5	N/A
Masonry support	C&S engineer	4	4	4
Curtain walling	Architect	4	4	6
Insulated render	Architect	4	4	6
Stone cladding	Architect	4	4	6
Louvres	Architect	5	5	N/A
Ceiling systems	Architect	5	5	N/A
Hot and cold water services	M&E engineer	4	4	6
Ventilation (natural and a/c)	M&E engineer	4	4	6
Sprinklers	M&E engineer	4	4	6
Electrical services	M&E engineer	4	4	6
Lifts	M&E engineer	4	4	6

Notes:

1. The example above looks solely at Stage 4. A completed Design Responsibility Matrix (DRM) for Stages 2, 3 and 4 should be completed at Stage 1 for incorporating into the professional services contracts.

2. Classification references are not shown. It is anticipated that these will be developed 'below the bonnet' with mapping between systems, such as Uniclass, Omniclass and NRM, allowing greater use of the terms above for different purposes until a common classification system is developed.

4. A notes column would be added to the completed DRM to allow a finer granularity. For example, for masonry support it might show the architect as responsible with the C&S engineer providing supporting advice and calculations. The design responsibility column may also be bolstered by adding a column that defines support roles. This would be of particular use on the largest of projects.

5. **Level of detail (LOD)**
The level of detail in the 'analogue' version of the DRM in *Assembling a Collaborative Project Team* used scale. Initiatives to shift LOD to a 'digital' format are under way and will be published in the spring of 2015. Updates will be available at www.nbs.com, where the attributes for this column will be considered in greater detail. For the purposes of this example, LOD is defined as follows:

4. Design intent information for use by specialist subcontractor – produced by the design team

5. Information for construction (including offsite manufacturing) – produced by the design team or the specialist subcontractor

6. Information for CAFM purposes – produced by the design team or the specialist subcontractor

6. **Level of information (LOI)**
The LOI primarily relates to the specification and data. The LOI acknowledges that the descriptive to prescriptive journey finishes at Stage 4 with either a design team member or specialist subcontractor providing the prescriptive information used for construction and/or In Use purposes. In the example above, the specialist subcontractor LOI is not indicated. Where the design team is assigned LOI 4 the prescriptive specification will be undertaken by the subcontractor. Where the design team is assigned LOI 5 there are no subcontractor design responsibilities and the design team information is prescriptive and suitable for construction purposes.

Figure 4.1   Extract from a completed Design Responsibility Matrix (incorporating Information Exchanges) showing Stage 4 responsibilities

How will the Project Strategies change during Stage 4?

Project Strategies have different purposes at different stages. During Stages 2 and 3 they contain a level of detail commensurate with the core design work. Too much detail results in the lead designer having too much information to review. Indeed, if the level of detail is too advanced, the lead designer may not have sufficient context to allow them to make informed comments. At Stage 2 the Project Strategies are an essential part of communicating the Concept Design to the client, and during Stage 3 they assist the coordination process.

At Stage 4, many of the Project Strategies will become defunct, their Stage 3 contents used to prepare Stage 4 Technical Design information. It needs to be made clear that certain project strategies have no role to play in Stage 5. For such project strategies the Stage 3 content will need to be sufficiently robust and unambiguous to allow those preparing the Technical Design to easily interpret and use them in the preparation of their own design. For example:

❙ The Maintenance and Operational Strategy should clearly state where water and power supplies are required for cleaning equipment to be provided by the client. Where a cherry picker is proposed for window cleaning, the loadings and the areas where it will run need to be clear to the engineer designing the sub-base.
❙ The Sustainability Strategy will need to have moved from general high-level aspirations to specific recommendations. For example, does it state how many bird boxes are required and where they will be located?
❙ The acoustic strategy will need to be prescriptive in relation to noise reduction requirements for walls and doors. These requirements will be incorporated into the specification for the windows and used in the selection of the most appropriate wall build-up, allowing partition details to be prepared.

These points underline the need for the lead designer to ensure that all of the Project Strategies are aligned prior to Stage 4 commencing. The lead designer should also ensure that the project lead has included in the Schedules of Services for those producing any Project Strategies concluded at Stage 3 a requirement to clarify aspects or provide further but limited contributions during Stage 4.

The core Project Strategies contained within the RIBA Plan of Work 2013 continue to be relevant during Stage 4 and are refined accordingly. These are considered below.

What drives the Design Programme during Stage 4?

Procurement is by far the biggest influence on the Stage 4 Design Programme, fundamentally determining the amount of overlap between the design work of the design team and that of the specialist subcontractors with design responsibilities. The impact of different procurement routes is considered further below. There are a number of other independent but related aspects that drive the framework for this stage's Design Programme. In particular, the Stage 4 Design Programme is influenced by:

I the period allocated within the Project Programme
I the procurement strategy, and how it dictates and determines Stage 3, 4 and 5 activities
I the extent of design work being undertaken by specialist subcontractors
I the scale and complexity of the project
I the sector involved (a hospital has more technical complexities than a community centre)
I whether any new and innovative features need to be integrated into the design
I design dependencies.

While procurement may be the biggest driver in setting the strategic dates in the Design Programme, design dependencies have the greatest influence on its content, particularly from the lead designer's perspective. Both subjects are now considered further.

Integrated Design Programme

An integrated Stage 4 Design Programme is one that contains the design activities of both the design team and the specialist subcontractors. This integration allows the lead designer to obtain core design information earlier in the process, helping them to overcome the challenge of integrating the design work of the specialist subcontractors. Examples of where this would be of benefit are covered in the section on design dependency (see page 126).

How does procurement influence the Design Programme?

While the Stage 4 tasks of the design team and of the specialist subcontractors appointed by the contractor remain broadly the same from project to project, the procurement route impacts the timing of when these tasks are undertaken. This section outlines the impacts of different procurement routes on the Stage 4 Design Programme, solely from the lead designer's perspective, starting with the procurement routes that achieve the best results.

Contractor-led

From a Stage 4 perspective, contractor-led procurement creates the most integrated Design Programme approach. The design team is part of the contractor's team from the outset and the supply chain is more likely to contribute to the holistic effort. Where the contractor has received preferred bidder status at the beginning of Stage 3 (with a view to the Building Contract being placed at the end of the stage) they are likely to persuade their specialist subcontractors to provide focused contributions to the Stage 3 coordination exercises. Whether or not this is the case, they will all be appointed prior to Stage 4 in a manner that allows the preparation of a single and integrated Stage 4 Design Programme.

Two-stage design and build

A core benefit of two-stage design and build procurement is that the contractor is appointed at an early stage, allowing them to contribute to strategic design and coordination decisions during Stages 2 and 3, on matters such as the type of structural frame or the sort of lifts to be used. However, as their own commission is limited in its nature they may not secure the same supply chain contributions from their specialist subcontractors. Stage 4 efforts are typically divided into two tranches. The effort prior to Building Contract award is rightly focused on cost clarity and risk reduction using partial Stage 4 information. There will be input from both the design team and the specialist subcontractors into the Contractor's Proposals which will be incorporated into the Building Contract. The design team will have remained on the client side during this first tranche, which dilutes the contractor's ability to influence its outputs. In the second tranche of effort, post Building Contract award, the design team will be novated to the contractor (although not always

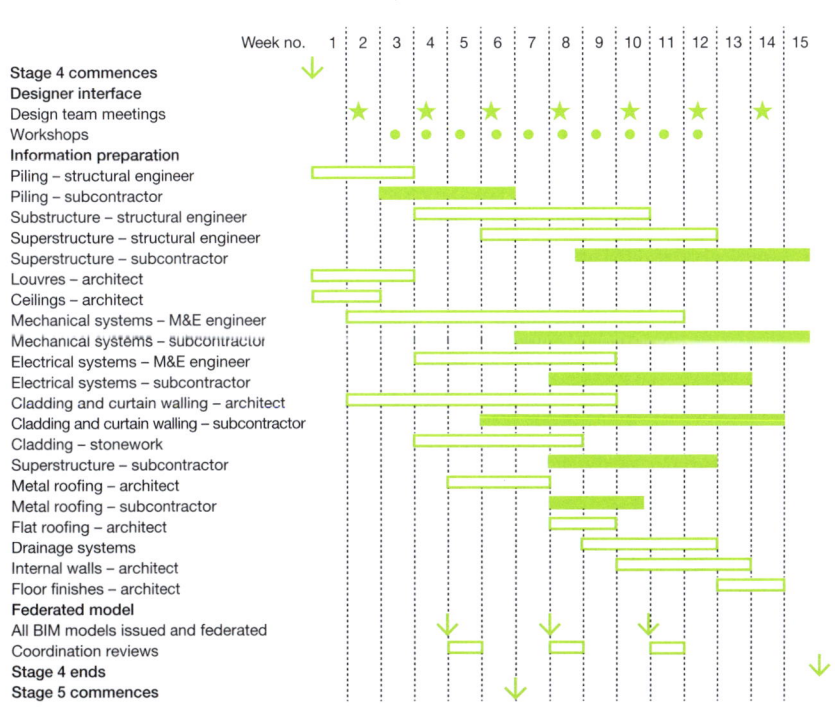

Figure 4.2 *Extract from a contractor-led project Stage 4 Design Programme*

Notes:

1 Review of information is incremental and by element and is not shown.
2 Cost activities removed. The contractor may undertake these but they do not fundamentally alter the lead designer's work and as such they are not included in the Design Programme.
3 Programme shows design work of the design team and specialist subcontractors and generally follows construction activity.
4 Construction (Stage 5) commences on completion of piling information.
5 For clarity, not all building aspects are shown.

the full design team) and the lead designer will produce an integrated Design Programme. The amount of information sitting on either side of the divide will vary from project to project, and many decisions may already have been made before the Building Contract has been concluded, creating an environment that is not ideal from either the lead designer's or the contractor's perspective. This can make the completion of Stage 4 challenging.

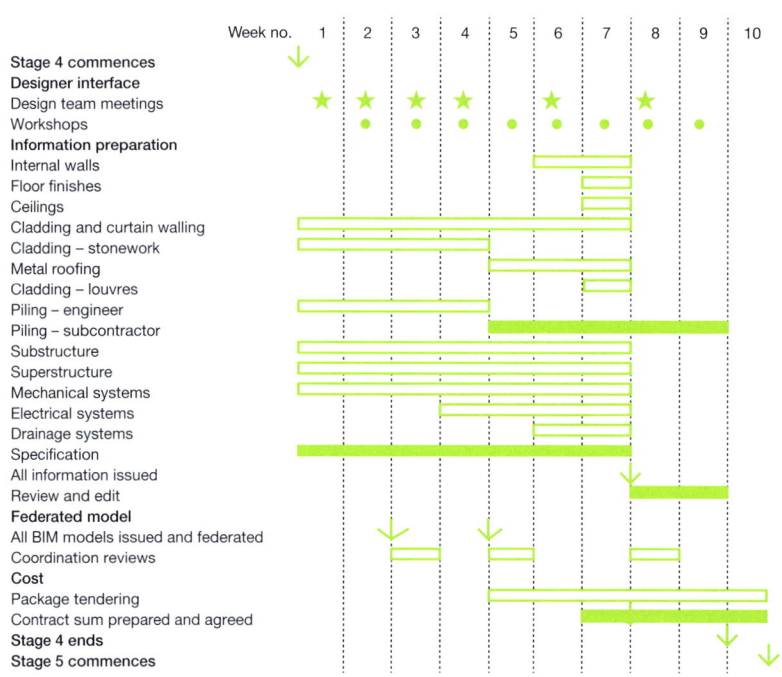

Notes:

1   10-week design period has been structured to allow an early start on site yet allowing the contract sum to be based on as much information as possible.

2   Single review period shown at the end, including a final BIM coordination review, although there is not much time available for a comprehensive review and tenders have been issued. The review allows risk allowances to be determined.

3   Design information is focused on initial construction packages (to construction status) as well as those covering risk. The specification is highlighted as it will need to cover aspects that are not drawn in detail prior to the award.

4   Everyone is working concurrently and design dependencies will be more difficult for the lead designer to manage. Design team meetings (as well as workshops) are shown as weekly in the early weeks to provide additional management of these issues.

5   The design programme shows only the design team information produced for agreeing the contract sum. A separate and integrated design programme would be prepared after the award of the Building Contract covering the remaining design team aspects and the specialist subcontractor design elements. An early award of the piling package has been undertaken to allow the specialist subcontractors' design work to be concluded to allow a start on site immediately following agreement of the contract sum.

Figure 4.3   Extract from a two-stage design and build Stage 4 Design Programme

Management contracting

In theory, management contracting allows the preparation of an integrated Design Programme in a similar manner to contractor-led procurement. Two core differences of this form of procurement are that the design team remains part of the client's team throughout and, more importantly, the

Construction Programme drives the procurement programme, which in turn drives the Design Programme and the release of information to the contractor in packages. The former difference should not be problematic where a collaborative project team is formed, although it does put certain aspects of decision making outside the contractor's direct control. The latter difference is crucial from the lead designer's perspective. While an integrated Design Programme can be created, the need to prioritise construction and procurement activities means it is inevitable that the Design Programme will contain design tasks that are undertaken outside of their 'natural' sequence. Examples could include:

I the main frame and handrails for precast stairs being designed and tendered after the stairs have been constructed (the stair design would need to be suitably robust to allow for the handrail brackets)
I the detailing and specification of flooring systems after loading assumptions have been made and the frame erected. For example, the structural engineer may have assumed raised flooring in an area but the architect may require a screed to accommodate the specified finish.

If the construction process is to occur without any serious buildability issues, the lead designer, as well as the design team members and the contractor, will need to have experience of designing out of sequence. For example, the lift car interior could be the first drawing issued for construction purposes, and it might be another 12 to 18 months before the final pieces of information in place, at which point the construction will have been substantially progressed. This substantial overlap of design and construction underlines the design challenges inherent in this form of procurement, particularly from the lead designer's viewpoint.

One-stage design and build

The challenges presented by one-stage design and build projects will depend on the Information Exchange used for tendering. Stage 3 information is commonly used, with perhaps some items that would typically be undertaken at Stage 4 incorporated into it. Some clients may have a preference for using Stage 2 information, allowing the contractor to give input at an earlier stage, including contributing to Stage 3 coordination exercises with their specialist subcontractors. While this does allow risk to be transferred earlier, the flip side is that the cost allocations for risk, due to the limited level of detail available, can impede the early agreement of a contract sum.

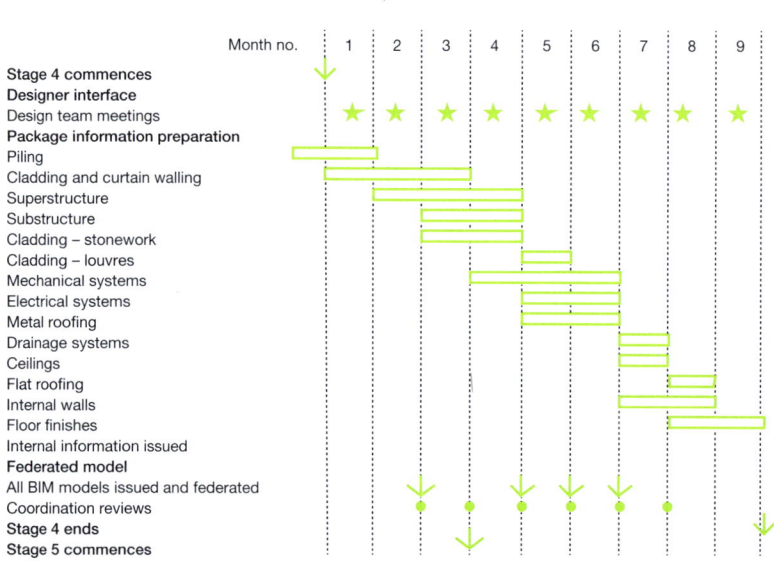

Figure 4.4   Extract from a management contract Stage 4 Design Programme

This scenario creates different risks for the lead designer. Where Stage 3 information is used to form the Employer's Requirements and the Contractor's Proposals are substantially unchanged from the Employer's Requirements – the contractor having had limited, if any, ability to contribute to the design development – the priority for the lead designer is to accurately and carefully present the status of each aspect of the design within the tender documentation so that the appropriate risk allowances can be made. Following award of the Building Contract, the lead designer can prepare an integrated Design Programme. The challenges will be to bring the novated design team members, the contractor and the specialist subcontractors together in a short period of time and to deal with the likely pressure to achieve an early start on site date.

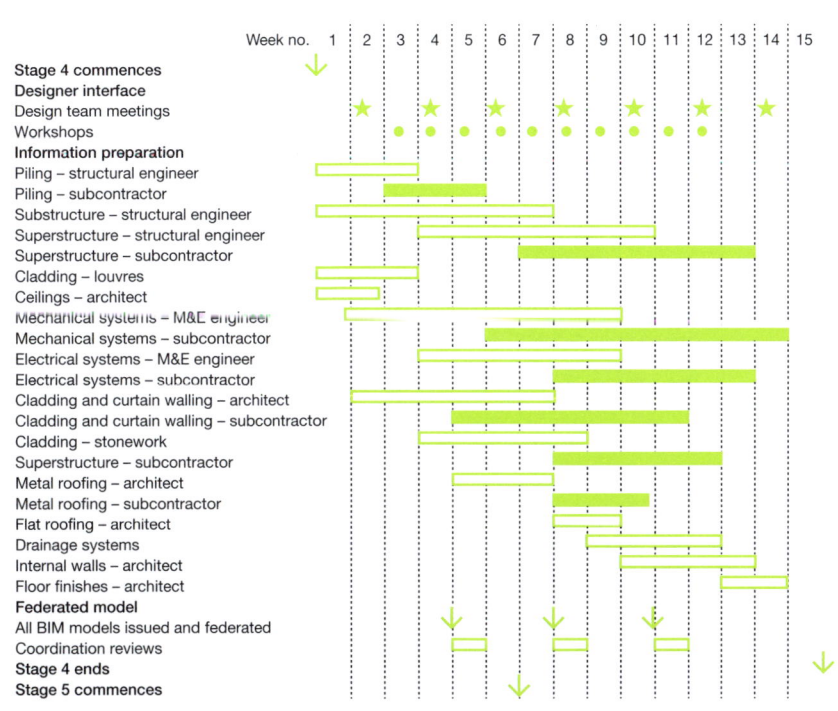

Stage 4 commences
Designer interface
Design team meetings
Workshops
Information preparation
Piling – structural engineer
Piling – subcontractor
Substructure – structural engineer
Superstructure – structural engineer
Superstructure – subcontractor
Cladding – louvres
Ceilings – architect
Mechanical systems – M&E engineer
Mechanical systems – subcontractor
Electrical systems – M&E engineer
Electrical systems – subcontractor
Cladding and curtain walling – architect
Cladding and curtain walling – subcontractor
Cladding – stonework
Superstructure – subcontractor
Metal roofing – architect
Metal roofing – subcontractor
Flat roofing – architect
Drainage systems
Internal walls – architect
Floor finishes – architect
Federated model
All BIM models issued and federated
Coordination reviews
Stage 4 ends
Stage 5 commences

Notes:

1 Review of information is incremental and by element and is not shown.

2 The Building Contract was awarded immediately prior to Stage 4 commencing and cost activities have therefore been removed. The contractor may undertake these but they do not fundamentally alter the lead designer's work and as such they are not included in the Design Programme.

3 Programme shows design work of design team and specialist subcontractors and generally follows construction activity.

4 Construction (Stage 5) commences on completion of piling information.

5 The programme is similar to the contractor-led programme, the exception being that the early packages for site are compressed (design team and specialist subcontractor) to facilitate a prompt start on site.

6 For clarity, not all building aspects are shown.

Figure 4.5   Extract from a one-stage design and build Stage 4 Design Programme

Traditional procurement

Traditional procurement requires two Design Programmes: one for the preparation of Stage 4 information by the design team for inclusion in the tender documentation, and one for the completion of any Contractor's Designed Portion (CDP) design work undertaken by a specialist subcontractor following award of the Building Contract. The main challenge from the lead designer's perspective is that certain aspects of what the design team produces would benefit from specialist subcontractor input. While such advice can be sought, it is typically non-binding, non-contractual and, as the specialist subcontractor has not been appointed to the project, may be provided at a superficial level. The bottom line is that it is common for design information prepared on the basis of such discussions to require reconsideration once the contractor is appointed.

Contractor's Designed Portion (CDP)

A crucial consideration relating to design responsibility is understanding how the design boundaries between the design team and any specialist subcontractors are affected by the choice of procurement route. With design and build and contractor-led forms of procurement, the contractor is responsible for all aspects of the design. The boundaries between the design team and the specialist subcontractors are determined by who is best placed to undertake the design, as set out in the Design Responsibility Matrix. With traditional procurement, the principle is no different. However, any aspect of the design that is to be allocated to a specialist subcontractor needs to be defined as a 'Contractor's Designed Portion' in the Building Contract. Under this type of contract, the design team remains responsible for the rest of the design.

The Design Responsibility Matrix includes an additional column for use on traditional projects to make sure that any CDP items are clear from the outset, allowing the design team to prepare its Stage 4 information accordingly.

In extreme situations this may require the coordinated design to be adjusted and an instruction to be issued, incurring additional costs and perhaps leading to an extension of time. For this reason, the extent of CDP work should be kept to a minimum on a project under traditional procurement. Where this is not possible, the lead designer should ensure that the contract administrator has made appropriate contingencies within the Project Budget and Project Programme to allow for the additional costs and programme time dictated by this form of procurement and the inevitable need for instructions.

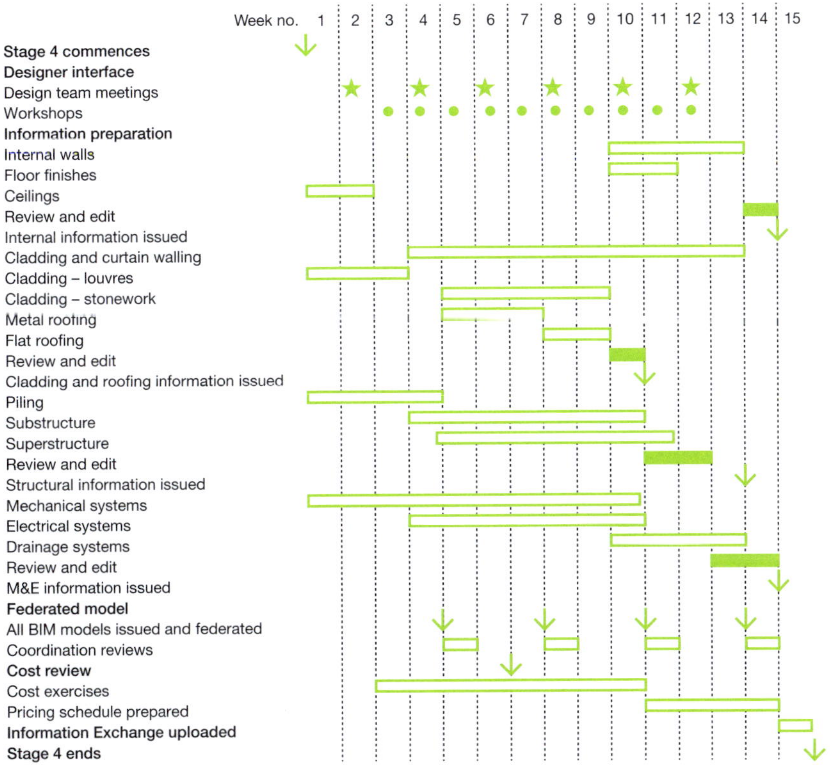

| | Week no. | 1 | 2 | 3 | 4 | 5 | 6 | 7 | 8 | 9 | 10 | 11 | 12 | 13 | 14 | 15 |

Stage 4 commences
Designer interface
Design team meetings
Workshops
Information preparation
Internal walls
Floor finishes
Ceilings
Review and edit
Internal information issued
Cladding and curtain walling
Cladding – louvres
Cladding – stonework
Metal roofing
Flat roofing
Review and edit
Cladding and roofing information issued
Piling
Substructure
Superstructure
Review and edit
Structural information issued
Mechanical systems
Electrical systems
Drainage systems
Review and edit
M&E information issued
Federated model
All BIM models issued and federated
Coordination reviews
Cost review
Cost exercises
Pricing schedule prepared
Information Exchange uploaded
Stage 4 ends

Notes:
1 The review periods will depend on who is reviewing – in this instance it is assumed that it is solely the lead designer. The architectural reviews are reduced to reflect the practice's internal processes.
2 Cost excercies and a Stage 4 cost report are shown. On many projects pre-tender estimates are not undertaken.
3 The architect is producing ceiling and louvre information first, to allow M&E information to progress, and is then focusing on the cladding

packages, where the greatest amount of coordination is required. The architectural team is programmed to complete the internal packages after that.
4 The completion of information is staggered to allow the lead designer adequate time to review each 'package'.
5 The design programme shows only the design team information produced for tender.
6 There is no overlap with Stage 5. The tendering process can begin when Stage 4 ends.

Figure 4.6   Extract from a traditional project Stage 4 Design Programme

Different procurement routes are unlikely to create different demands on the lead designer during Stages 2 and 3, except as set out in the previous two chapters. However, during Stage 4 different procurement routes create substantially different challenges for the lead designer, who needs to be mindful of these when considering the tools that might be used to overcome them.

What other purposes does the Stage 4 Design Programme serve?

As set out above, the strategic contents of a Stage 4 Design Programme are determined by the procurement route. The Design Programme might not schedule every design dependency that is identified (see the following section), but the lead designer will need to make sure that the general thrust and direction of design activity align with such requirements. For example, there is no point in the Design Programme stating that the architect will produce ceiling layouts during September if the mechanical engineer's programme suggests the layouts are required during August. It is typical for a Stage 4 Design Programme to be based on the core Technical Design activities of each designer, such as cladding information or ceiling information etc.

The Design Programme can also be a crucial tool for determining and allocating resource requirements.

It is not common to have intermediate reviews of Stage 4 information or for client presentations or reports to be produced. Therefore, from a meetings perspective, the Design Programme can be simpler, although it is useful to include design team meetings and workshops so that these can be aligned with core production periods, to allow reporting or the rapid resolution of any issues that may arise during the process.

What are design dependencies and why are they crucial?

A design dependency is an element of the design that must be completed by a designer before another designer can progress their design work. Design dependencies exist during Stages 2 and 3; however, these are more transparent and relate to high-level aspects of design and coordination. Although most designers are able to progress the majority of their work independently during Stage 4, it is inevitable that at least one designer will require information from another to allow them to progress. Examples of design dependencies include the following:

  I The M&E engineer will need ceiling layouts in order to place lights, grilles, sprinkler heads, smoke detectors and other items.
  I The design of exposed steelwork connections will require the architect's specific visual requirements and the structural engineer's specific structural requirements.

| The M&E engineer will need to know details of the lift car interiors or how glass-backed lifts are to interface with other aspects of the design.
| The structural engineer will need to know kerb details and manhole cover specifications to complete information for the external works (eg are finishes to be integrated into the covers?).

Some of these dependencies will require 'mini' iterations. For example, when the M&E or C&S engineer proposes products or specifications, the lead designer or architect may pass back comments that require another option to be considered or other items to be considered. The lead designer should continue to use the design status schedule during Stage 4 to ensure that the various items identified in the Design Programme or during the stage continue to be flagged up until they have been concluded. As this is likely to be a detailed list, the ability to split the design status schedule down into subcategories, typically by role, is essential.

In some sectors, such as healthcare or laboratories, experience of the design dependences likely to be encountered can be invaluable. It will help the lead designer to be proactive rather than reactive.

What other tools would the lead designer use during Stage 4?

The design status schedule can be used to record ongoing design issues as they are addressed and resolved during Stage 4. However, it needs to be remembered that the issues in this schedule cannot be dealt with by the developing information or emails (see the following topic) alone. The lead designer will need to arrange workshops to address particular points as they arise and as the relevant information is produced. With the specialist subcontractors on board, design team workshops need to be refocused if they are to be effective. The best method of doing this is to ensure that all of the designers have the dates for the workshops in their diary, but that the agendas are left 'loose' until a few days before the meetings. This will allow the most important topics to be addressed. Also, the invite list should be edited down so that only those who need to contribute are involved. Each meeting might be split into a number of sessions to provide further focus.

Why is email the enemy of the lead designer during Stage 4?

Direct communication has not been touched on so far. During Stages 2 and 3, design team meetings and workshops form the backbone of the

Design status schedule

Date raised	Date last discussed	Raised by	Item raised	Action required and/or status	Priority	Action by (date)	Action by (who)	Status
22-Aug-14	22-Aug-14	Arch	Sub-base for toilet floors to be finalised. Options include plywood on raised floor, blockwork laid on side and lightweight screed.	Contractor to confirm preference for sub-base to allow architect's information including specification to be finlaised.	1	28-Feb-15	Cont	Live
22-Aug-14	12-Sep-14	M&E	Sprinklers' heads can be 'pop-down' or exposed below the ceiling.	Architect has confirmed preference for pop-down heads. Cost consultant to advise on any cost implications.	2	N/A	CostCon	Live
29-Aug-14	12-Sep-14	Arch	RAL colour availability for exposed fire-protected steelwork to be confirmed.	C&S engineer to confirm RAL availability.	2	22-Feb-15	C&S	Live
12-Sep-14	12-Sep-14	M&E	Options for light fittings to canopy have been issued to architect.	Architect to confirm preference for light fitting.	3	22-Feb-15	M&E	Live
22-Sep-14	22-Sep-14	Arch	Agreed that cabling for canopy light fittings can be concealed within steelwork. Location of distribution board in entrance hall needs to be reconsidered.	M&E engineer to discuss potential cable routes with C&S engineer and suggest alternative distribution board locations.	3	28-Feb-15	Arch	Live

Figure 4.7   *Stage 4 design status schedule*

design-making processes outside of the design development undertaken by each design team member.

During Stage 4 it is crucial that the lead designer does not allow an email culture to prevail. In its worst form, such a culture results in too many emails going to too many people (but, ironically, not to the right people). Furthermore, tracking and monitoring such emails can be time consuming and counterproductive. The lead designer needs to establish mechanisms that allow queries to be raised and answered and comments to be made on design information as it is produced. The design status schedule can be used to record design dependency and other coordination and integration issues, where they can be tracked and monitored until they are closed out.

What Cost Information is considered during Stage 4?

On most forms of procurement the contractor will be progressing Cost Information prior to Stage 4, and in many instances will already be under contract. Where Cost Information is produced during Stage 4 it will typically be by the contractor's subcontractors, including the specialist subcontractors, although the cost consultant will be responsible for vetting and validating such information. On a traditional procurement project, it used to be commonplace to undertake pre-tender estimates. This now occurs less frequently, because of the time required to do so and due to the simple fact that the contractors' tenders set the real benchmark for the costs associated with the design team's Stage 4 information.

What drives the specification during Stage 4?

Three types of specification are used at Stage 4:

I Prescriptive
The design team is responsible for the design and specifies specific and particular products. The design team is unlikely to be interested in considering alternatives put forward by the contractor because the client may have signed off specific products or set out specific requirements in the Initial Project Brief. Alternatively, the planning consent may have specified the use of particular materials.

I Descriptive
The design team remains responsible for the design, but specifies in a manner that allows the contractor to select certain products.

This approach might be used for 'hidden' items, such as wall ties or damp-proof membranes, giving the contractor the option of sourcing the most suitable products from their supply chain. The design team remains responsible for the final selection and so needs to review and approve any products proposed by the contractor. In some instances, reference products might be included in the specification. The contractor need not use these but should take note that these meet the quality standards expected.

Performance

Where the contractor and, in turn, the specialist subcontractor will be responsible for the design, it is typical to deliver geometric design intent information. In a similar vein, the specification will use performance clauses to give greater guidance regarding the parameters to be used when the design is produced.

It is essential that the lead designer understands the different types of specification that can be used and ensures that they are used appropriately. The form of procurement does not necessarily impact on the type to be used, although a greater amount of descriptive specifying would be expected on design and build contracts and a greater proportion of prescriptive specifying on a traditional project. Procurement does not necessarily determine the boundary between the design team and the specialist subcontractor; however, it is essential that the specification is geared accordingly, with the performance clauses giving the specialist subcontractor the right basis on which to start their design work.

Design intent

Where the design team will hand the design baton over to the specialist subcontractors at Stage 4 the design team will prepare design intent information. This information will be more detailed than Stage 3 information and will give design guidance where required. The right level of detail is crucial. Too little information will not provide enough guidance, but too much may prevent the specialist subcontractor from innovating and will create inefficiencies in the overall design process.

Another topic that the lead designer needs to consider at Stage 4 is who will review the various drawings that are produced. On a traditional project, the design team's inputs would normally be reviewed only by the lead designer. On a design and build or contractor-led project, others may need to review the information, including the contract administrator. The same would apply to the drawings produced by the specialist subcontractors, although the lead designer might also require other designers to review these. It is crucial that the lead designer understands who needs to review what. It can be beneficial to include the anticipated review periods in the Design Programme to alert any reviewers to the likely timescales.

What procurement activities are necessary at Stage 4?

Figure 4.8 highlights the remaining procurement activities to be undertaken during Stage 4. The previous section has already noted that with one-stage design and build, management contracts and contractor-led procurement, the Building Contract will have been signed and the team will be working in an integrated manner. The previous section also noted the different impacts of two-stage design and build and traditional procurement on the timing of preparing Stage 4 information and the associated Design Programme implications. All forms of procurement will be concluded at some point during Stage 4, prior to construction commencing on site during Stage 5.

What influences the Project Programme at Stage 4?

The Project Programme should already contain the timescales required to suit the selected procurement route. Stages 4 and 5 will always overlap, regardless of the procurement route. The procurement route and Project Programme will define the extent of overlap, with management contracting creating the greatest overlap.

It is possible, however, that issues will arise in agreeing the contract sum or the contractor may require a longer mobilisation period. Additional time may be required to deal with such issues. Conversely, the contractor may be able to reduce the construction period, although in such instances the client may wish to retain any float within the Project Programme.

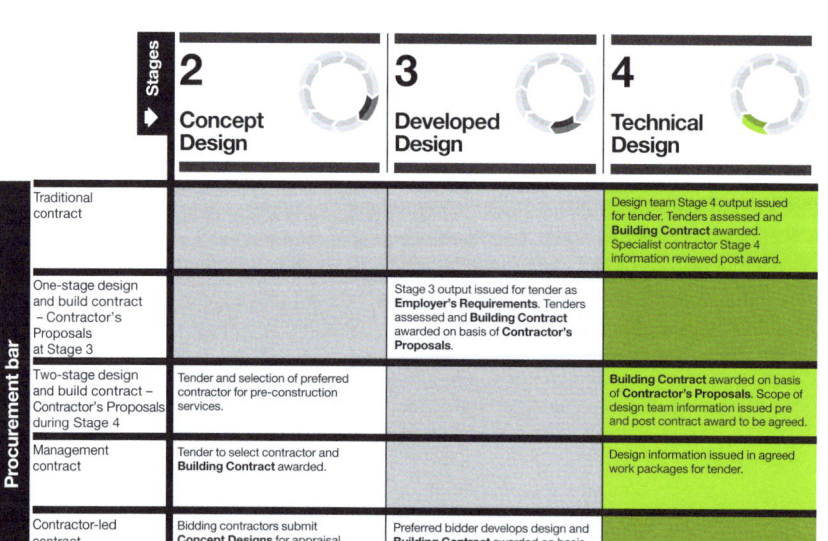

		2 Concept Design	3 Developed Design	4 Technical Design
Procurement bar	Traditional contract			Design team Stage 4 output issued for tender. Tenders assessed and **Building Contract** awarded. Specialist contractor Stage 4 information reviewed post award.
	One-stage design and build contract – Contractor's Proposals at Stage 3		Stage 3 output issued for tender as **Employer's Requirements**. Tenders assessed and **Building Contract** awarded on basis of **Contractor's Proposals**.	
	Two-stage design and build contract – Contractor's Proposals during Stage 4	Tender and selection of preferred contractor for pre-construction services.		**Building Contract** awarded on basis of **Contractor's Proposals**. Scope of design team information issued pre and post contract award to be agreed.
	Management contract	Tender to select contractor and **Building Contract** awarded.		Design information issued in agreed work packages for tender.
	Contractor-led contract	Bidding contractors submit **Concept Designs** for appraisal.	Preferred bidder develops design and **Building Contract** awarded on basis of **Contractor's Proposals**.	

Figure 4.8   Procurement activities during Stages 2 to 4 for different procurement routes (Stage 4 highlighted)

Another matter that may impact on the Project Programme is the planning consent. The Stage 3 Information Exchanges will be used for the planning application, and while pre-application discussions and meetings are likely to have been held, there may be reasons beyond the control of the project team that result in changes being required or, in the worst case scenario, consent not being granted. There will be a significant delay as the application goes through the appeal process or a fresh application is made. In the worst case scenario, the client may choose to abort the project.

Where the planners require adjustments that will be dealt by the local planning authority under delegated powers the client may wish the design team to progress at risk to minimise any delays. The design team should be cautious in such situations and be clear that any further adjustments as a result of ongoing negotiations will be subject to further Change Control Procedures. The lead designer should consider the risks and advise the team accordingly. For example, changing one elevation from render to stone may have little impact on the design team, but plan adjustments may impact on the work of the entire design team.

With so many diverse variables to be considered, each project needs to be considered individually. Good programme management by the project lead should allow any adjustments required for issues typically encountered to be made using the programme contingency without affecting the overall Project Programme period.

How does town planning influence Stage 4 design management?

Planning consent will typically have been granted by the time Stage 4 commences. The core issue for the architect, project lead and lead designer is to ensure that any planning conditions that impact on Stages 4, 5 and 6 are properly addressed and, where appropriate, incorporated into the Building Contract. Issues typically encountered will relate to the contractor's site operations at Stage 5, such as site compound layouts, noise, waste and other logistical issues. Issues to be addressed by the lead designer might include:

I ensuring that plant configurations do not exceed noise emission criteria
I specifying windows that comply with noise reduction criteria
I producing sample panels for sign-off.

A planning conditions tracker can be a useful tool for ensuring that the planning conditions are being dealt with during Stage 4 and beyond. It is also a useful mechanism for conveying the status of such information at design team meetings.

What supporting tasks should be undertaken during Stage 4?

The Suggested Key Support Tasks at Stage 4 comprise the following:

I Review and update Sustainability, Maintenance and Operational and Handover Strategies and Risk Assessments.
I Prepare and submit Building Regulations submission and any other third party submissions requiring consent.
I Review and update Project Execution Plan.

I Review Construction Strategy, including sequencing, and update Health and Safety Strategy.

During Stage 4 the majority of support tasks relate to the updating of Project Strategies produced during Stage 3. As outlined above, some Project Strategies will have been completed at the end of Stage 3 and will be in use by the design team to assist the preparation of the Technical Design Information Exchanges. The core strategies in the Suggested Key Support Tasks task bar are considered further below.

How might the Sustainability Strategy change at Stage 4?

The Sustainability Strategy might be tweaked during Stage 4, but the core priority, which is underlined in the Sustainability Checkpoints, is to ensure that any formal assessment processes have been completed, details audited for compliance with the strategy and Building Regulations aspects closed out.

What influences the Maintenance and Operational Strategy at Stage 4?

The Stage 3 Maintenance and Operational Strategy should be sufficiently robust at Stage 4 to allow the Technical Design proposals to be developed without impacting on any of the strategies that have been set out, although, as the Technical Design progresses, the strategy should continue to be tested. For example, more detailed studies in relation to the cleaning of roof lights may require a different cherry picker, with different loads and dimensions, to be considered. This change would need to be factored into the Technical Design and will require adjustments to the Maintenance and Operational Strategy.

What drives the Handover Strategy at Stage 4?

The Technical Design of the M&E services is the item most likely to result in refinements to the Handover Strategy during Stage 4, as the design is progressed to the next level of detail. Furthermore, because Stage 4 includes the work of the specialist subcontractors, it is likely that items requiring further consideration will arise. One other point to consider is that on the majority of procurement routes the contractor will be appointed at the start of or during Stage 4 and negotiations may require adjustments to the Handover Strategy and/or the Project Programme in relation to commissioning periods or other core aspects.

How do Risk Assessments alter at Stage 4?

During Stage 4 any risks are likely to be transferred to the contractor. Typical exceptions include risks related to statutory consents – planning consent in particular – where the cost of risk transfer might be disproportionate to the perceived risk. It is likely that such risks will remain at a high level, therefore the project lead will probably retain management of them through to completion, using their own Risk Assessments.

From the lead designer's perspective, most risk will have been converted to sums included within the contract sum or, in the event of traditional procurement, retained as contingencies. The procurement section above highlighted the benefits of the lead designer setting out the status of such risks in a design status schedule. The lead designer should continue to monitor such risks during Stage 4 until they are concluded.

What third party submissions may be necessary?

Planning consent should be obtained prior to Stage 4 commencing. The main consent to be achieved during Stage 4 is Building Regulations approval. Where this is being undertaken by an independent practice, rather than a local authority, it is advisable to have some checks undertaken during Stage 3 to ensure that the building plans are robust at the beginning of Stage 4. Regardless of the route, the information required for such a submission should be developed and submitted as early as possible during the stage to minimise the potential for abortive work.

Some of the third parties listed in the previous chapter may not be able to progress their consents or sign-off processes during the previous stage or concurrently with the planning application. By Stage 4, any remaining consents should require only 'rubber stamping', with initial discussions having been held to minimise any risks. However, these consents should certainly remain a high priority as part of any Risk Assessments. A priority for the project lead and the lead designer is to ensure that all of the necessary consents have been identified and that they are submitted as early as possible. This will minimise the impact on Stage 4 tasks of any issues that need to be addressed.

What should the Construction Strategy consider at Stage 4?

More detail will be added to the Construction Strategy during Stage 4, as the contractor is appointed and the work of the specialist subcontractors progresses. The contractor is likely to have more detailed discussions with specialist subcontractors on sequencing and other matters that will inform the development of the Construction Programme during Stage 4. Method statements will begin to be developed and, while they might not all be incorporated into the Construction Strategy, they may need to be referenced and the Construction Strategy adjusted accordingly. As issues are examined in greater detail, particularly in relation to sequencing, the lead designer needs to make sure that if any assumptions made to date are altered, the Construction Strategy is reviewed accordingly.

> **What aspects might the Health and Safety Strategy consider at Stage 4?**

During Stage 4 it is likely that the Construction Strategy will deal with the majority of health and safety issues. One crucial consideration is that the lead designer will hand over responsibility to the contractor at some point in time. The contents of the Health and Safety Strategy will need to be adjusted to reflect this and the ongoing nature of the Stage 4 design activity, which will be undertaken in conjunction with Stage 5.

While Stage 4 sees the completion of the design information to be used for construction during Stage 5, it is important to remember that the information at the end of Stage 5 ('As-constructed' Information) is more important from a health and safety perspective, particularly in relation to the In Use phase.

What Information Exchanges occur at Stage 4?

The Information Exchange at Stage 4 is the completed Technical Design of the project.

Defining the Technical Design is straightforward: it is the optimum information required in order to construct, maintain, operate and use the project. There are, however, a number of major complexities:

I design teams have historically focused on producing information for construction, not for other new purposes
I there is no industry or sector guidance on what constitutes best practice or 'optimum' information

| there are no agreed boundaries between what the design team designs and what the specialist subcontractors design, although 'common practice' exists for certain aspects
| some elements might be capable of being designed by various designers and/or require contributions from different designers
| BIM and other digital technologies are fundamentally changing the way information is produced
| due to the overlap with Stage 5 there is no formal conclusion of Stage 4
| deliverables requirements are commonly framed in a drawing-based, not model-based, manner.

This guide does not consider what constitutes 'optimum' or best practice as initiatives are under way that will begin to bring clarity on this subject. It is heartening that these initiatives are focused on the information required for the whole life cycle of a project (Stages 0 to 7), on achieving a common understanding of who does what, and on how to define Information Exchanges in a digital environment. These initiatives will drive consistent and clear Information Exchanges in the future. In the meantime, the lead designer needs to consider the following issues:

| The design work of the design team and lead designer needs to be better integrated. How can this be achieved, other than via new procurement models?
| Design processes need to be altered to drive better integration, with design-to-manufacture processes driving design and programme efficiencies.
| 2D information will still have to be produced for some time (using traditional techniques or derived from the BIM model), such as for site operatives when setting out prefabricated components, or for bricklayers (see below).
| Different procurement routes will create different 'lines in the sand'. How can these best be managed, and what need will there be for 'intermediate' Information Exchanges for contractual purposes?

Due to the overlap with Stage 5 it is not common to have a formal Stage 4 Information Exchange as information is issued incrementally in accordance with the Design Programme. The next chapter considers how this information might be incorporated into the Stage 5 Information Exchange.

BIM and 2D information

2D information can be produced it two ways in a BIM environment. The first is that it can be 'sliced' from the BIM model, using processes that create files that can be shared in a number of common formats. Plans, sections and elevations can all be produced using this process. Because drawing sets are produced from a 'single source of truth', there is no possibility of contradictory information. The 'slices' can be defined and set up at an early stage, minimising the timescales for this work.

One point to consider is that reviewing and design management processes are also moving into a digital environment, harnessing the BIM model directly – as a result, the need for such 2D information is reducing, although the need for new and innovative processes is increasing.

Less frequently discussed is the 2D information produced from 'flattened' BIM files. This would occur where the 2D information generated by 'slicing' does not contain sufficient detail without additional drafting and/or notes, in 2D, to supplement the level of detail derived from the BIM model. This technique is used, for example, where the architect is responsible for producing Stage 4 information for construction purposes rather than for use by a specialist subcontractor. While the 2D information is akin to 'traditional' 2D CAD information, it does contain intelligence from the BIM model, minimising the risk of incorrect information being produced.

This subject is not widely discussed and, clearly, where a design team produces such information for construction purposes they should be compensated accordingly. This further underlines the importance of the Design Responsibility Matrix.

Chapter summary 4

The Design Responsibility Matrix and Design Programme are
crucial tools during Stage 4 and must properly reflect the subtle
nuances of the selected procurement route. The lead designer
needs to consider the differing demands of different procurement
routes and adjust the lead designer role accordingly. The aim of
Stage 4 is to have the right information available at the right time:
first, to allow the specialist subcontractors to undertake their
design work and, second, to allow Stage 5 activity to commence on
or off site. The increasing integration of design teams allows the
lead designer to consider Stage 4 more holistically and to produce
a Design Programme where the work of the design team and the
specialist subcontractors is dealt with more holistically.

Construction

Chapter overview

Design work is completed during Stage 4, with the exception of responding to any Design Queries that may be generated by the contractor. During Stage 5 the work of the lead designer will depend on the Schedule of Services that has been agreed and included in their professional services contract and, in part, on the procurement route. This chapter considers what tasks the lead designer might undertake at Stage 5 and, more crucially, what lessons might be learned from current construction trends and how Stage 5 knowledge might be harnessed to help practices and clients improve their processes in the earlier project stages.

The key coverage in this chapter is as follows:

What are the Core Objectives of Stage 5?

What procurement activities occur at Stage 5?

Why might the Project Programme change at Stage 5?

What tasks related to town planning are required at Stage 5?

What supporting tasks should be undertaken during Stage 5?

What Information Exchanges are common at Stage 5?

Introduction

At Stage 5 the contractor takes centre stage. The contract administrator role is also pivotal because the Building Contract requires instructions to be issued as well as monitoring to ensure that the contractor is proceeding as intended, as set out in the contract documents. On smaller projects the architect typically undertakes this role; however, on larger contracts different parties may undertake this role, depending on the procurement route.

Stage 5 includes offsite manufacturing and onsite construction undertaken in accordance with the Construction Programme. The differences between these different forms of construction and their relationship to the Construction Programme are considered below. It is crucial to note that the design cannot be 100% complete at Stage 4; however, the only design-related activity that occurs at Stage 5 is responding to Design Queries arising from site operations. This subject is considered further on page 148.

The RIBA Plan of Work 2013 emphatically places the design work of specialist subcontractors into Stage 4. While the Project Programme will typically determine that this work is undertaken in parallel with Stage 5, it is not part of this stage. Stage 5 is focused solely on construction. The lead designer has no real role in Stage 5 activities, although they may remain involved in the project due to the overlap of Stage 4 activities. In addition, they may be best placed to respond to Design Queries due to their holistic understanding of the coordinated and integrated design. The lead designer may also need to be consulted if changes to sequencing, as set out in the Construction Strategy and Construction Programme, are proposed or where change is initiated.

A final area that may also benefit from the involvement of the lead designer is site quality. The party appointed to undertake regular quality inspections on site will vary depending on the procurement route. Due to their holistic understanding of the design, the lead designer is well placed to undertake such reviews, where the procurement route permits. Even in scenarios where the lead designer is novated to the contractor, it is commonplace for a client to request that the lead designer produces a report for inclusion in the contractor's monthly progress report.

Practical Completion triggers the end of Stage 5 and the issues associated with this are of greatest interest to the contract administrator. The activities dictated by the Handover Strategy, however, are of greater interest to the lead designer. These are considered further in the next chapter.

What are the Core Objectives of this stage?

The Core Objectives of the RIBA Plan of Work 2013 at Stage 5 are:

With the specialist subcontractors' design work carried out during Stage 4, a crucial consideration during Stage 5 is the relationship between offsite and onsite construction and the drivers for greater use of the former. It is also important to understand why Design Queries arise on site. All of these subjects are considered in greater detail below.

How do offsite manufacturing and onsite construction differ?

The RIBA Plan of Work 2013 acknowledges the increasing use of offsite construction and the important role that this will increasingly play on future projects. Prefabrication is already commonplace in some sectors. For example, on new hotels the use of prefabricated rooms is becoming the 'norm', but in large open-plan office developments, the drivers are different. However, on all project types an increasing number of components, such as the structural frame, staircases and cladding components, are prefabricated.

Some clients value other benefits of offsite construction, such as the ability to reduce the amount of disruption caused when building on a constrained site. Indeed, some university or hospital estates will include offsite construction as a core requirement in the Initial Project Brief.

Offsite construction has a number of other potential benefits. It can:

I improve quality, as repetitive processes are carried out under factory conditions
I reduce site time, when harnessed with traditional construction (for example, an insitu substructure used with a precast concrete frame)
I reduce health and safety risks, especially where works are being undertaken in the winter when weather, light and temperature issues create challenges on site.

Transportation is often a limiting factor for the use of prefabrication. Module sizes can reach the limits allowable for transportation on the road network, limiting the timing of deliveries and possibly increasing the need for police escorts, making transportation expensive.

Common prefabricated components include:

I precast cladding panels, perhaps using special concrete mixes with carefully selected stone, pigments and, possibly, mica, and sometimes with stone or brick facings
I panelised curtain walling panels, typically one storey high by one main structural bay wide
I precast concrete frames with precast floor panels
I services preassembled on trays to reduce erection time.

The lead designer needs to be mindful of all of these different developments as they impact on the coordination work at Stage 3 and, in some instances, may need to be considered strategically at Stage 2. It is essential that the Construction Strategy initiated at Stage 2 reflects the extent of offsite fabrication possible. Other trends are emerging, such as:

I Large-scale buildings are increasingly being modularised in factories. Hospitals in the Middle East are good example of this. The requirement to build in 'double walls' on a constant grid creates new design demands, different from those for fixing a grid for a steel, timber or concrete frame, and so becomes a Stage 2 driver.

I The use of onsite factories is increasing, where larger modules are fabricated on site and then craned into position. This approach enables raw materials, such as coiled steel, to be delivered directly to site for fabrication, reducing and simplifying transportation costs.

I The use of robotic machinery for both onsite and offsite manufacturing is increasing. The cost of such machines is decreasing and their functionality is increasing. With labour costs rising, a tipping point will occur, resulting in the use of robotic equipment becoming more commonplace, both on site and off site.

As these diverse trends become more commonplace, the Construction Strategy will have even greater importance at Stage 2. The lead designer needs to keep abreast of such developments so that their suitability is properly considered by the project team as early as possible. For example, a building constructed using a structural frame requires a column grid, whereas room modules require bigger wall zones creating more constraints. These are crucial and strategic design drivers.

One conundrum is that different contractors have different approaches and supply chains and may suggest different solutions in different circumstances. While the lead designer might incorporate the use of offsite construction into the Developed Design and have it referenced in the Construction Strategy, factors outside their control may change the strategy and require the design to be modified to include less or more prefabrication. One of the benefits of early contractor engagement is that the Construction Strategy is likely to be better considered and more robust

How does the Construction Programme differ from other forms of programme?

The Construction Programme is a core tool for the contractor. It performs a number of functions at different stages. For example, it enables the contractor to:

I during the tender period, check and ratify that the construction period included in the Project Programme is realistic and achievable

I consider sequencing of the various works and understand where pinch points may occur during the construction process

I prepare subcontract programmes for inclusion in tender documents issued to subcontractors and for incorporation into any subcontract documents following their agreement

I examine the critical path and the areas that would cause significant delays should any issues arise on site

I monitor actual progress on site against planned progress and report on this progress at regular intervals.

It is crucial that the lead designer comments on the Construction Programme at the appropriate times. The Construction Programme produced at tender stage might be a 'first stab' and so not merit close inspection, but the first version issued following the award of the Building Contract will need to be examined in detail. While the lead designer may not have the skills or experience necessary to comment on every aspect of the programme, they will have a good understanding of the design. As a result, they may be able to identify sequencing issues, such as problems arising where elements do not dovetail because of how they have been detailed. For example:

I the partitioning might be detailed in a manner that requires partitions to be erected before screeding activity can commence

I some walls may only need to be built up to ceiling level, requiring the ceiling to be in place first

I brickwork might be detailed in a manner that requires it to be in place before the curtain walling to achieve waterproofing.

The primary purpose of the Construction Programme is to dictate the logic and timing of construction activities. The contract administrator will monitor monthly progress against the Construction Programme included in the Building Contract. Where the contractor makes an application for an extension of time, the contract administrator will need good programme skills to be able to analyse the delay and respond to the claim.

What are Design Queries?

In an ideal world no Design Queries would be generated from site – the contractor would be able to construct the works without any additional design input after Stage 4. It is certainly true that increasing the proportion of offsite construction and/or the use of specialist subcontractors (who need to produce more detailed information, typically called 'shop' drawings, for their own activities on site) reduces the number of Design Queries. However, the reality is that unexpected issues will be encountered, particularly in relation to the site itself and the assumptions made around it. For example:

I additional services may be discovered once ground has been broken on site

I ground conditions may not be as expected or old foundations or other anomalies encountered, requiring the substructure to be adjusted

I information from different designers may be contradictory, requiring one party's information to be amended (establishing a BIM environment will minimise this possibility).

While some of the initiatives set out in this guide will help ensure that the right information is delivered at the right time, a pragmatic approach is also required. The bottom line is that it is inevitable that some Design Queries will arise on site due to the many variables inherent in any project, relating to the site, the brief and the client, among other things. In some instances, Design Queries might stem from a lack of knowledge regarding what is required or intended: do you really want to do that? The lead designer also needs to understand that the design team has been 'living and breathing' the design for a long time whereas the contractor may not have had the opportunity to understand the rationale behind many design decisions. Design Queries are typically referred to as RFIs (requests for information) or TQs (technical queries). A successful project team will have clear and established processes for dealing with Design Queries, rather than responding to them in an ad hoc manner.

What procurement activities occur at Stage 5?

The procurement activities of the RIBA Plan of Work 2013 are solely focused on the administration of the Building Contract at Stage 5. The party best placed to undertake the contract administrator role will vary depending on the procurement route and the scale and the complexity of the project.

The Building Contract could be based on one of a number of different standard forms of contract in common use. It is therefore important that the contract administrator has experience of administrating the form used on the project. One crucial element of the contract administration role is to ensure that quality on site is reviewed against the specification and drawings incorporated into the Building Contract. Again, it is essential that anyone who undertakes the review of quality on site is experienced in doing so. Historically, the design team member responsible for preparing the Stage 4 information would have carried out this role, but, with novation of them to the contractor commonplace, the client and contract administrator need to consider who is best placed to undertake this role.

Why might the Project Programme change at Stage 5?

The Project Programme may need to be altered at the beginning of Stage 5 to dovetail with the contractor's Construction Programme included in the Building Contract. Where handover is crucial to In Use activities, for example, a university facility being handing over for occupation at the beginning of a new academic year, it is crucial for float to be included in the Project Programme. This should be in addition to any float that may be 'hidden' within the Construction Programme. As construction nears completion, if it is anticipated that the building is to be handed over late, or even early, the client may need to prepare a 'mini' programme to consider revised timings for fit-out works or other aspects that might be undertaken post handover and in order to coordinate other activities included within the Handover Strategy.

What tasks related to town planning are required at Stage 5?

During Stage 5, a number of conditions may need to be discharged by the contractor. Most of these will relate to matters such as recycling, site compound details, noise that might be generated by plant or restrictions on when work may take place. Some of these may have been incorporated into the Building Contract and may have been discharged prior to construction commencing.

On a conservation project, samples of workmanship may have to be prepared on site for approval by the local authority planners. Such requirements should be agreed between the architect and the contract administrator, accepting that in many circumstances these roles might be undertaken by the same practice.

What supporting tasks should be undertaken during Stage 5?

The Suggested Key Support Tasks at Stage 5 comprise the following:

❚ Review and update the Sustainability Strategy and implement the Handover Strategy, including agreement of information required for commissioning, training, handover, asset management, future monitoring and maintenance and ongoing compilation of 'As-constructed' Information.

❚ Update Construction and Health and Safety Strategies.

The supporting tasks at Stage 5 divide into those that assist the construction process, such as the Construction Strategy and the relevant sections of the Heath and Safety and Sustainability Strategies, and those that help with the handover of the building.

What is the purpose of the Sustainability Strategy at Stage 5?

The Sustainability Strategy at Stage 5 will mainly deal with the onsite activities of the contractor, such as the control and reduction of waste materials. The importance of these aspects cannot be overstated, and they are core considerations in many sustainability accreditation schemes.

When should the Handover Strategy be implemented during Stage 5?

The issue of the certificate of Practical Completion signals the end of construction and Stage 5. However, the Handover Strategy commences before Practical Completion and therefore bridges Stages 5 and 6. This overlap would be included in the Project Programme and the period will depend on the complexity of the Handover Strategy. To commence the implementation of the Handover Strategy, a number of activities need to be undertaken during Stage 5, including commissioning activities and training of staff. The Handover Strategy is considered in greater detail in the next chapter.

What is 'As-constructed' Information?

'As-constructed' Information is a core Information Exchange during Stage 5 and is considered in the Information Exchanges section below.

What alters the Construction Strategy during Stage 5?

While the Construction Strategy developed and updated during Stages 2 to 4 should be relatively static during Stage 5, it is likely that, once construction commences, situations will be encountered that require the Construction Strategy to be fine-tuned. The document is intended to be dynamic, like all the other strategies on the project. For example:

I a safer methodology for constructing an element of the works might be proposed by a subcontractor's squad on site
I sector best practice might have moved on and new methods should now be used
I new equipment or plant and improved construction methodologies might be available
I new legislation might have been implemented that must be addressed.

The lead designer may need to be consulted on certain changes to the Construction Strategy if changes to coordinated or integrated information are required. It is more likely that an individual designer will need to be consulted if a change in strategy has an impact on only their design proposals.

What alters the Health and Safety Strategy during construction?

In a similar vein to the Construction Strategy, the Health and Safety Strategy should be considered a live document. The contractor and any design team members involved during Stage 5 should be alert to possible improvements to health and safety matters. Some contractors promote initiatives such as monthly awards to encourage greater consideration of health and safety issues. Most health and safety initiatives during Stage 5 relate to the protection of construction workers, covering matters such as site access and temporary protection, and do not generally require the involvement of the design team or the lead designer.

Are Change Control Procedures still valid during construction?

The RIBA Plan of Work 2013 does not include a reference to Change Control Procedures at Stage 5 because making any change during this stage would have significant cost and programme implications. It is recommended that no change is made at this stage, except in exceptional circumstances. It is, of course, possible that the client will instruct changes at Stage 5.

In some sectors, such as retail (when the tenant has come on board), some changes during Stage 5 are likely to occur. The Change Control Procedures set out in Stage 3 remain valid and should be used. The contract administrator is best placed to lead this process, using cost advice from the cost consultant. In some instances, a design proposal may need to be developed to allow a change to be properly costed. It is crucial that those preparing such proposals sit outside the project team preparing the Stage 4 information (which will be happening concurrently in such instances). With construction work ongoing, it can be challenging to provide fixed costs for a change and, of course, time becomes crucial as more work is constructed. It is feasible that further costs will be incurred between the initiation of a possible change and its instruction.

Those managing the process also need to consider the Construction Programme – the contractor should not to place areas on hold because a change might occur. A potential change remains such until it is emphatically instructed by the contract administrator.

What Information Exchanges are common at Stage 5?

The Stage 5 Information Exchange comprises the 'As-constructed' Information. Three items need to be considered in relation to this:

How is 'As-constructed' Information defined?

The core issue at Stage 5 is to define what will constitute 'As-constructed' Information. This is not a straightforward consideration because ratifying every single piece of information would require a substantial amount of work. This is because the design team does not supervise construction and cannot therefore state that the works 'as constructed' are the same as the works 'as designed', even if there is a fair and reasonable chance that they are. The same principle applies to the specialist subcontractors who supervise their own work, because adjustments to their work may have been required in response to issues that arose on site. That said, they are more likely to issue 'As-constructed' Information, whereas the design team will typically issue its final construction issue set.

As it is feasible that works are not constructed in accordance with the Stage 4 design information, particularly in relation to geometric aspects (for example, walls may have been erected in slightly different locations to those indicated in the designer's information), the client must decide how accurate the information needs to be for future use as well as what information is required.

This point needs to be considered at Stage 1, so that the requirements can be incorporated into the various contracts. The following questions should be asked:

I Will the last version of the federated PIM model (as issued for construction) be sufficient?
I Will the accuracy of the last federated PIM model be sufficient or will greater accuracy be required?
I If greater accuracy is required, how will this be achieved? (see below)
I Does the information need to be updated to take account of Design Queries?
I Is all of the Stage 4 information required? If so, in what format?
I Will the information be used for computer-aided facilities management (CAFM) or asset information purposes? If so, what information and formats are required?

It is important to understand that these are crucial considerations at Stage 1 as they will have a major impact on the fees involved and on the client's ability to use the information handed over. In terms of accuracy, a point cloud survey would ratify as-constructed wall positions, but such an exercise would be an unnecessary expense if this degree of accuracy is not required. The project lead needs to consider such aspects and determine the appropriate level of detail for each project. This will form the Stage 5 'As-constructed' Information, which should be defined in the Handover Strategy at Stage 1.

Where 'As-constructed' Information is to be transferred into CAFM or asset management software systems, the timing of the transfer needs to be considered. This will depend on the items noted above, although certain data will need to be added to such systems prior to occupation. This is an important point to consider because the information has a 'new start' once it is imported into the CAFM or asset management system – at this point it is frequently referred to as the 'project information model' (PIM), the information used throughout Stage 7 until the end-of-life phase.

What Stage 4 information should be incorporated?

A vast majority of the Stage 4 information will be produced solely for construction purposes. It is not standard practice to issue all of this information to the client. In a BIM environment it becomes easier to hand over more information, and such information can be invaluable

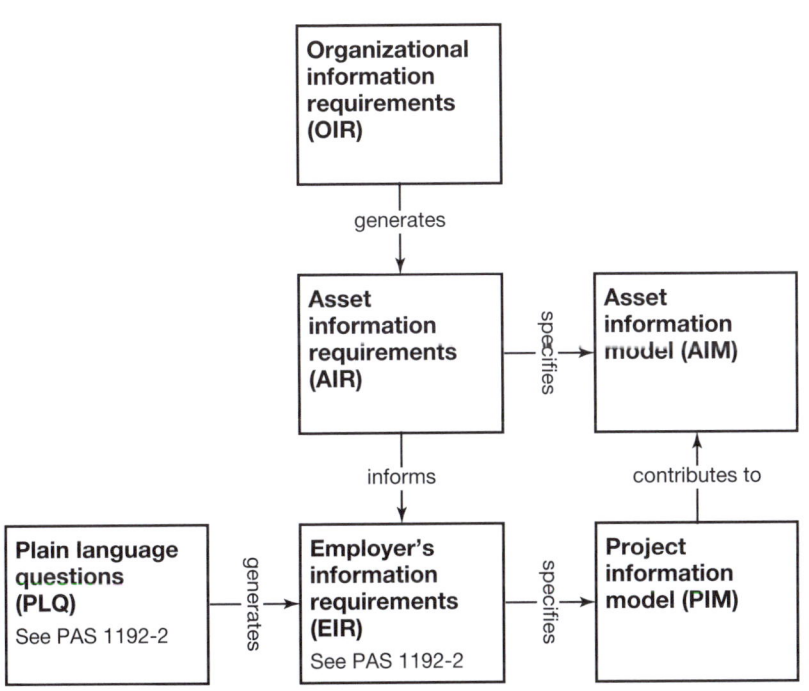

Figure 5.1   How the PIM relates to the AIM as set out in PAS 1192-2

if alterations to the building are required. The federated PIM should certainly be included, along with all of the data required for CAFM or asset management software systems. However, such information needs to be caveated if it is not categorised as having 'As-constructed' Information status.

How should Design Queries be dealt with?

A review of Stage 4 information may be required to ensure that the responses to any substantial Design Queries have been incorporated into the Stage 5 information. While this is not common, it is an important topic to be considered.

Chapter summary 5

Stage 5 focuses solely on construction activities. An increasing amount of construction work is now being undertaken off site, which improves quality and health and safety aspects, and can even reduce the overall construction period. However, as the balance of work swings from on site to off site, the contractor is required to consider different issues, and it may impact on the work of the lead designer at Stages 2 and 3 who has to meet the demands of designing for fabrication. The contract administrator role has also become more complex, due to the different demands of the various procurement routes and standard forms of Building Contract in use and because of considerations centred around site quality. The final complication for the construction phase is how to ensure that the lead in to Practical Completion and handover is properly considered. This is dealt with in the next chapter.

Handover and Close Out

Chapter overview

The Handover Strategy takes centre stage during Stage 6, as construction comes to end and the process of handing over the building to the client, who may also be the user of the building, commences. The activities that need to be carried out prior to occupation have become more complex over the years. Increasingly, clients understand that if a building is to operate effectively and as designed, this stage is crucial and needs to be undertaken diligently. The increased complexity of handover requires activity to occur before and after Practical Completion and the process will vary from project to project, depending on the sector, scale and complexity.

The key coverage in this chapter is as follows:

What are the Core Objectives of Stage 6?

What procurement activities occur at Stage 6?

Why might the Project Programme change at Stage 6?

What town planning activities occur at Stage 6?

Why are the supporting tasks crucial at Stage 6?

What Information Exchanges might take place at Stage 6?

Introduction

Stage 5 emphatically ends with Practical Completion – the issues associated with this were covered in the previous chapter. Stage 6 also ends in a similar emphatic manner, with the issue of the final certificate closing out the Building Contract. The beginning of Stage 6 is much softer, focusing on the activities that will create the best possible start to a client's use of a building. The diverse nature of the two ends of Stage 6 results in two strands of activity: those associated with closing out the Building Contract and those that are part of the Handover Strategy which was developed and defined during Stage 1. The Building Contract aspects will be managed by the contract administrator, but other roles may be best placed to manage the tasks set out in the Handover Strategy.

The overlap between Stage 5 and Stage 6 is a deliberate intent of the RIBA Plan of Work 2013. This overlap is essential if a building is to function as intended. At the end of Stage 5 the contractor and contract administrator will be focused on achieving Practical Completion on time. Their focus is likely to be on contractual matters rather than dealing with the tasks set out in the Handover Strategy, the latter being of greater interest to the client. Therefore, other project team members might concentrate on the Handover Strategy, separately from those whose primary concern is Practical Completion. Indeed, having a team that is focused solely on the post-occupancy phase makes it more likely that the client's Project Objectives will be achieved.

An effective Handover Strategy can benefit all projects and all project team members, but is important to consider who will be best placed to deliver the strategy at Stage 6. The team responsible for delivering the requirements of the Handover Strategy will vary depending on the client and the project size and complexity. For example, clients with an internal estates team, such as a university, may be best placed to lead the handover team and drive the Handover Strategy to completion.

It is unusual for the lead designer to have any duties during Stage 6, although a defect might arise that requires the lead designer's overview rather than the opinion of an individual design team member. The contract administrator will need to be mindful of this and may need to consult with the lead designer on receipt of the snagging lists from the individual members of the design team. The lead designer may also be required to undertake their own inspection on a more strategic level. In reality, because the architect is likely to be from the same practice as the lead designer, this scenario is not frequently encountered.

What is of greater interest to the lead designer is the changing nature of project handover arising from the use of ever more complex systems in buildings and a greater understanding of why buildings do not behave as anticipated and designed. It is difficult to ascertain how the lead designer role will change as handover processes become more refined and integrated into Building Contracts, but as a number of issues are likely to be multidisciplinary and require references to be made to earlier design stages and information, it is arguable that the role will increasingly become more important, indeed essential, during Stage 6.

What are the Core Objectives of this stage?

The Core Objectives of the RIBA Plan of Work 2013 at Stage 6 are:

Stage 6 of the RIBA Plan of Work 2013 deliberately avoids reference to Practical Completion, which is triggered by the completion of construction at Stage 5. However, it does refer to conclusion of the Building Contract, which typically triggers the end of the contractor's involvement in the project at the end of Stage 6.

Stage 6 is therefore a hybrid stage. At the start it is focused on the Handover Strategy and, as it nears conclusion, on the Building Contract.

What other activities related to the Building Contract occur during Stage 6?

The core focus at the commencement of Stage 6 is resolving the snagging items identified at the end of Stage 5. These can range in scope and scale and therefore the timescales for concluding them can also vary. The snagging list should not typically take long to close out. Where the list is comprehensive, the contractor should provide a programme identifying when remedial work will be carried out. This can be essential where the building is already operational.

The purpose of the defects liability period, triggered by Practical Completion, is to ensure that the building has properly bedded in, that works highlighted on the snagging list have been identified and that any latent defects that have been identified are resolved. An amount of retention is allowed for in the cost valuations (which determine payments to the contractor) to act as an incentive to the contractor to close out the snagging list during the defects liability period, and also to act as a contingency should they choose not to rectify any of the defects identified. The *RIBA Plan of Work 2013 Guide: Contract Administration* considers these issues in greater detail.

While all of these activities are of little interest to the lead designer, there are benefits in understanding the reason for defects occurring. Feedback may improve Stage 4 design information on future projects.

What procurement activities occur at Stage 6?

The procurement activities during Stage 6 of the RIBA Plan of Work 2013 are closely related to the Core Objectives and require the contract administrator to facilitate the conclusion of the Building Contract.

It is feasible that, in the future, changes to handover processes will lead to a new generation of Building Contracts. It is also possible that during Stage 6, new procurement activities will take place to facilitate the operational management of the building, such as a tender for facilities management.

Why might the Project Programme change at Stage 6?

It is not essential to update the Project Programme during Stage 6, although it may need to be updated to reflect the actual completion date as this, in turn, determines the likely date for issuing the final certificate. It may also be beneficial to update any dates related to the Handover Strategy or periods of time identified by the contractor for resolving and concluding the defects (snagging list) that were identified at Practical Completion.

What town planning activities occur at Stage 6?

No specific town planning activities are required during Stage 6.

Why are the supporting tasks crucial during Stage 6?

The Suggested Key Support Tasks at Stage 6 comprise the following:

I Carry out activities listed in the Handover Strategy including Feedback for use during the future life of the building or on future projects.
I Updating of Project Information as required.

What is the purpose of the Handover Strategy at Stage 6?

Traditionally, the end of Stage 5 focuses on completing a project by the contractual completion date. Delays can make this process fraught and the contractor and the contract administrator are likely to be focused on this contractual process. The Handover Strategy, in contrast, focuses on the activities that will make the building more effective from a user's perspective (sometimes the user is the client, but in other instances the user is a client of the client). Many activities need to be undertaken to ensure that an effective handover is facilitated as construction nears completion:

I the building services need to be commissioned (with seasonal commissioning carrying on for a year)
I users need to be trained in the use of systems contained within the building; for example, how to use a new electronic room-booking system, how to operate the building management system (BMS) or, in a high-end residential refurbishment, how to operate the home cinema and its sound system
I manuals need to be prepared to advise the client how to maintain and operate the building
I following occupation, members of the design team should be present to advise on how the building can be run more successfully; for example, are the windows being operated in line with the Sustainability Strategy (they may need to be opened at night to cool the exposed concrete structure) or is the FM team experiencing issues with any of the systems.

Handover Strategy

The value of the Handover Strategy tasks in ensuring the successful operation of a building is increasingly being appreciated by clients. The lead designer should stress their importance in ensuring that key features of the building work properly. Further details of all of these activities and how they might be dealt with are included in BSRIA's Soft Landing guidance (www.bsria.co.uk/services/design/soft-landings/free-guidance/).

More specific information on the UK government's process for handing over a building can be obtained from the government's Soft Landings documents, which can be obtained at www.bimtaskgroup.org/gsl/.

How will the Handover Strategy process change in the future?

The shift towards handover processes that are focused on the user's needs rather than the needs of the Building Contract is still in its infancy, but significant developments in the future are inevitable. For example, with items such as seasonal commissioning now being commonly included in Building Contracts, it might be argued that Practical Completion should occur one year after beneficial occupation. Other initiatives suggest a three-year post-occupancy period to ensure that the users are using the building as planned and that the systems are working as designed. Such changes would also allow the client to incorporate measurable Project Outcomes into Building Contracts, such as the amount of energy consumed by a building. Maintenance obligations may also be included within this three-year period.

Why is Feedback crucial at Stage 6?

Feedback at Stage 6 would normally be focused on the project team's experiences as it is too early for operational Feedback on the building's performance. A Feedback session should be conducted as soon as possible after the end of Stage 5, while everything is still fresh in everyone's minds. Furthermore, project team members move on to new and separate projects very quickly and so it may not be feasible to gather everyone together again after even a short period of time.

What Project Information would be updated during Stage 6?

During Stage 6, a university may have already carried out stage activities, such as altering space planning layouts or carrying out minor room adjustments. These would be undertaken within the asset information model (AIM). Some adjustments to the AIM might be 'mini' Stage 0 to 7 projects in their own right, requiring further consideration on how to keep the AIM model up to date.

What Information Exchanges might take place at Stage 6?

There are no formal Information Exchanges at the end of Stage 6 as it is unlikely that any stage activity by the contractor will have impacted on the 'As-constructed' Information (PIM) issued at the end of Stage 5. However, if any changes are required to the AIM during Stage 6 as a result of concluding the Building Contact, a means of verifying them and integrating them into the AIM would be required.

Chapter summary   6

Stage 6 acts as the bridge between the commencement of Handover Strategy activities and the conclusion of the Building Contract. Two strands of activity occur at Stage 6: those associated with the Building Contract and those required to facilitate the successful occupation and running of the building. Both are of equal importance and neither would typically require the skills of the lead designer.

Stage 7

In Use

Chapter overview

The RIBA Plan of Work has historically ended with the conclusion of the Building Contract – the In Use stage of a building is making its appearance for the first time in the RIBA Plan of Work 2013. A core aim of the RIBA Plan of Work 2013 is to facilitate the capturing of high-quality data for use during Stage 7. New services will evolve around this data – in particular, it will increasingly be harnessed to inform the briefing stages of future projects, connecting Stage 7 to Stage 0. This will particularly benefit clients who repeatedly commission buildings, either for their own estate or for use by others.

The key coverage in this chapter is as follows:

What are the Core Objectives of Stage 7?

Why are no activities for procurement, programme or town planning included at Stage 7?

What are the purposes of supporting tasks at Stage 7?

What Information Exchanges might take place at Stage 7?

Introduction

In recent years many clients have focused more closely on the operational aspects of their buildings, particularly those who commission buildings on a regular and serial basis and certainly those who operate and maintain their own buildings. Such clients include airport operators, shopping centre developers and universities.

In many instances, these clients will have full-time facilities management (FM) teams, who understand the operational and maintenance requirements of their buildings. A client's FM team is likely to be involved in the briefing and design stages of a project to ensure that the proposals meet its own requirements. The Maintenance and Operational Strategy prepared at Stage 2 and updated during later stages is crucial for allowing the FM team to understand how the building will be maintained. More importantly, it allows the client to comment on and agree to the operational parameters that are defined during the design process, with the strategy acting as a record of this agreement. It is acknowledged that sometimes increased capital costs will result in reduced operating costs (OpEx) and that different maintenance solutions might be preferred by different FM teams.

The Handover Strategy is of equal importance to an FM team, as the design data that is handed over at the end of Stage 5 is increasingly being incorporated into computer-aided facilities management (CAFM) and asset management software systems, to be used when the building is handed over and becomes operational. This data will evolve and require updating during the life of the building. This is considered below.

Measuring Project Outcomes will become increasingly important as their contribution towards, and ability to reduce, total costs (TotEx) becomes clearer. Project Outcomes will only be improved if they are measured, benchmarked and then analysed before being harnessed for Stage 0 purposes on future projects.

Capital costs (CapEx) used to be the only core cost consideration on a project, but OpEx and TotEx are increasingly becoming central to clients' businesses. It is therefore imperative that the lead designer takes an interest in this project stage and understands the developing techniques and trends towards reduced OpEx (and the sustainability benefits of this) and better Project Outcomes. Indeed, in the multidisciplinary environment where all this work sits, it might be argued to the lead designer's skills will be crucial to success in this area.

What are the Core Objectives of this stage?

The Core Objectives of the RIBA Plan of Work 2013 at Stage 7 are:

At present, it is rare for a project team commissioned at Stage 1 to continue to provide professional services beyond Stage 6. The exception would be the Handover Strategy services that occur in years 1 to 3 post occupancy, when such services currently end. As the RIBA Plan of Work evolves in future years it is likely that these services will transfer into Stage 6 to take account of new practices in concluding the Building Contract. This chapter considers the current scenario, as well as setting out the services likely to be offered in the future, in the period following conclusion of the Handover Strategy through to the end of a building's life, when Stage 7 becomes a new Stage 0.

Why are no activities for procurement, programme or town planning included at Stage 7?

The procurement activities are complete by Stage 6 and so the Procurement and Programme task bars have no activities at Stage 6. Similarly, any planning issues concerned with conditions should have been closed out long before Stage 7. Therefore, these task bars are not relevant at Stage 7 and only the Suggested Key Support Tasks task bar activities are now considered. That said, clients may require Stage 7 services. Once the scope of these is better understood it can be determined if they might require Stage 0 activities in their own right (which would be the case, for example, for making internal modifications requiring the involvement of a designer and contractor).

What are the purposes of supporting tasks at Stage 7?

The Suggested Key Support Tasks at Stage 7 comprise the following:

I Conclude activities listed in Handover Strategy including Post-occupancy Evaluation, review of Project Performance, Project Outcomes and Research and Development aspects.
I Updating of Project Information, as required, in response to ongoing client Feedback until the end of the building's life.

The previous chapter noted that when a project team completes a building it is common practice for the team members to instantly move on to other projects, with the lessons learned rarely being discussed, recorded or properly considered for improving future Project Outcomes. The RIBA Plan of Work 2013 actively encourages the undertaking of any activity that can be harnessed to improve future work by the client, the design team and/or the contractor.

In the future, Project Outcomes will become more crucial as clients frame them in ways that allow them to be incorporated into the Building Contract. This will require ways of formally measuring on completion the Project Outcomes that were set when the Initial Project Brief was created. Design teams may have such outcome-based requirements included within their professional services contracts, either directly via the client or where they are appointed by the contractor. This will increase the need for all members of the project team to understand the briefing implications of Project Outcomes, how they may influence the Building Contract and the impacts if they are not achieved.

What is the purpose of the Handover Strategy at Stage 7?

As highlighted in the previous chapter, the Handover Strategy may contain tasks that take place in years 1 to 3 post Practical Completion (the end of Stage 5). The RIBA Plan of Work 2013 allocates these tasks to Stage 7, although they will be completed in the early years of a building's life. In the long term it is likely that these activities will transfer to a new and expanded Stage 6. Changes to Stage 6 of the RIBA Plan of Work 2013 will be considered when sufficient clarity and consistency of approach is established.

What is the purpose of a Post-occupancy Evaluation?

A Post-occupancy Evaluation is a systematic and rigorous evaluation of how a building is performing in use. It considers how well a building meets its users' needs, and can consider use from different perspectives, including those of staff, customers or operational teams. The data collected might be used to evaluate how effective the design has been in responding to the brief or, indeed, it may highlight improvements that might be used for future briefs. It can also be used as part of the fine-tuning process, where the building is adjusted in line with Feedback and other items of information. For organisations that embrace continual improvement processes it is a crucial activity to undertake.

Why is consideration of Project Performance crucial?

A review of Project Performance is a crucial aspect of any Post-occupancy Evaluation. It is not possible to ascertain how a building is performing until has been running for a while and its In Use performance is compared with the anticipated designed performance. This is particularly true for energy use. Initiatives such as CarbonBuzz (www.carbonbuzz.org) have highlighted the substantial performance gap between the two and the importance of this subject being considered and addressed in the broader Handover Strategy.

Why are Project Outcomes important at Stage 7?

Project Outcomes will play an increasingly important role on projects as they become better understood and categorised. They will eventually allow better and more intelligent briefing processes, as well as new ways of integrating such requirements into a new generation of Building Contracts. The measurement and benchmarking of Project Outcomes will become part of new Stage 7 to 0 activities, as highlighted elsewhere.

Why is consideration of Research and Development important?

Where Research and Development (R&D) has taken place on a project it is crucial that Feedback is obtained on the outcomes so that future projects can benefit from any lessons that were learned. In some instances, the R&D activity might be published, allowing clients or design team members to establish their innovation credentials within a specific sector. In other instances, R&D Feedback may be kept within a practice or business, but it will still need to be conveyed as part of a practice's continual improvement or knowledge management processes.

What Project Information should be updated during Stage 7?

A major transitional change, as outlined in the previous chapter, is that clients are increasingly harnessing the PIM for operational and In Use purposes. The asset information model (AIM) will continue to be updated until the end-of-life phase of the project. The information in the PIM will be used at the end of the building's life and will become part of the Site Information at Stage 0, regardless of whether the building is being demolished, refurbished or extended.

Why is Feedback important during Stage 7?

Most of the items identified in the sections above are all types of Feedback that can be obtained during Stage 7 and harnessed for future Stage 0 activity. Feedback can relate to any of the project stages. Feedback can be used to improve the efficient running or operation of a building, and clients can use it to improve their briefing processes and information on future projects.

What Information Exchanges might take place at Stage 7?

Once the 'As-constructed' Information (PIM) is incorporated into CAFM or asset management software systems it becomes part of the AIM. It will then continue to be updated in response to ongoing client Feedback and maintenance or operational developments. As the building nears the end of its life, this information can be used as the project moves from Stage 7 into a new Stage 0.

Chapter summary   7

Stage 7 is a new stage in the RIBA Plan of Work 2013. The lead designer will increasingly have an interest in this stage. Where they are not providing services related to this stage, they will have an interest in the activities of others, such as those undertaking R&D using data derived from the building or carrying out benchmarking exercises or evaluating Project Outcomes. Big data and the 'internet of things' will increasingly change the way that the spaces we use work and it is inevitable that these changes will lead to new briefing processes at Stages 0 and 1 and, in turn, to exciting new design approaches and processes at Stage 2 and beyond.

Design management glossary

Asset information model (AIM)

The term used to describe the PIM following its handover to the client for use in CAFM or asset management systems.

Asset management system

A software system used to assist the asset management of a building.

BIM

Building Information Modelling.

BIM model

A multidisciplinary design model prepared using BIM technologies. Reference would be made to the BIM model rather than the general arrangement drawings.

BREEAM

Building Research Establishment Environmental Assessment Methodology. A British sustainability accreditation scheme.

Briefing tracker

A document used to track changes between the Initial Project Brief and the Final Project Brief.

CAFM system

Computer-aided facilities management system – a software system used to assist the operational management of a building.

CapEx

Capital expenditure.

CI/SfB

A standard framework for the classification of architectural information. Used by the RIBA Product Selector.

Clash detection

The process of identifying clashes in a BIM model.

Clash free

A BIM model that has been reviewed for clashes, with any clashes having been identified and resolved – perhaps through a number of iterations.

Clash managed

A BIM model that is accepted despite the presence of clashes. A number of logical and understandable clashes can be accepted to avoid time-consuming adjustments within the PIM, for example floor boxes clashing with a raised floor system.

Common data environment (CDE)

A web-accessed portal where the current BIM information on a project can be reviewed or downloaded for use by any member of the project team. Typically, a third party provider would manage the CDE. This allows the independent verification of what was uploaded and when, if such information is required.

Construction cost

The contract sum incorporated into the Building Contract, as agreed between the client and the contractor.

Construction cost estimate

Prior to the receipt of tenders from contractors, the construction cost estimate is the cost consultant's estimate of the anticipated construction cost.

Contractor's Designed Portion (CDP)

Discrete elements of the design on a traditional contract for which the contractor takes design responsibility. Such elements will usually be designed by a specialist subcontractor.

Contractor's Proposals (CPs)

The contractor's response to the Employer's Requirements. The CPs will be incorporated into the Building Contract.

Coordination

The process of ensuring that the work of one designer fits with the work of all others. A coordinated design would contain no clashes.

Cost benchmark

Historical cost data used in the preparation of the Project Budget and/or the construction cost estimate.

Design dependency

An element of the design required from a designer in order for another designer to progress their work.

Design intent

A method of achieving a level of definition beyond which a specialist subcontractor will develop the work. The level of definition used for a Contractor's Designed Portion of the design.

Design manager

A role that involves managing the design process. It is not a design role, although it may be undertaken by a designer.

Design quality

The quality of design on a project. A design quality indicator or other methodology may be required to measure design quality or to compare projects in the same sector.

Design quality indicator (DQI)

A method of measuring design quality that takes account of the subjectivity in any assessment of design.

Design status schedule

A schedule used by the lead designer to manage the coordination and integration processes and to convey the current status of each aspect of the design to other project team members. The schedule can be used to convey design as part of the Employer's Requirements documentation.

Employer's Requirements (ERs)

The Employer's Requirements set out the basis of what the client is seeking to achieve on a design and build or contractor-led project. The Employer's Requirements can vary in geometric, data and specification content.

Federated model

A federated model contains all the design team BIM models. The models are reviewed by the lead designer before they are uploaded to the common data environment (CDE). Files related to the BIM models are also part of the federated model and can also be uploaded to the CDE. The federated model allows each designer to work with 'static' reference models as they produce their own design information and can allow different aspects to be progressed at the same time.

'Flattened' BIM file

A 2D extract taken from a BIM model in order to add a greater level of detail. The subsequent 2D drawing is produced in a conventional manner, but it has many of the attributes of and is linked to the BIM model.

Hot topics

Topics on a project that are frequently discussed and which require quick resolution to avoid them taking up a disproportionate amount of design management time.

Integrated Design Programme

A Stage 4 Design Programme in which the design work of the design team and the specialist subcontractors is collated into a single Design Programme, assuming that the procurement route allows the various parties to work together at the same time.

Integration

The process of adding the specialist subcontractors' information into the coordinated design.

Latent defect

A defect identified after Practical Completion that is not included on the snagging list but requires to be rectified under the terms of the Building Contract. Latent defects can also occur after the final certificate has been issued and after the contractor has left site.

LEED

Leadership in Energy and Environmental Design. An American sustainability accreditation scheme.

Level of detail (LOD)

LOD defines the extent of geometry that should be contained in a PIM or AIM at a given stage for each system, product and/or object. In certain circumstances the LOD for specific aspects might be produced at an earlier or later stage.

Level of Information (LOI)

LOI defines the fixity of the data (primarily specification) contained in the PIM or AIM for each system, product and/or object. In certain circumstances the LOI for specific aspects might be produced at an earlier or later stage. This is part of the descriptive to prescriptive journey.

Level of definition

A term used to define the amount of geometric and other data that should be contained in a BIM model. Different level of definition references require different levels of detail (LOD) and levels of information (LOI). Information Exchanges may require design information to be at different levels of definition at different stages.

Novation

The scenario where a design team or a design team member's professional services contract is transferred from the client to the contractor. The contractor becomes the new 'client'.

OpEx

Operating costs (expense) – the costs of running and maintaining a building (also referred to as whole-life costs).

PAS1192-2

A specification that sets out the methodology for producing a federated model in a common data environment, including the structure and processes required to facilitate this.

Plain language questions (PLQs)

Questions generated by the UK government's BIM Task Group to consider what the Information Exchanges might comprise at each stage.

Procurement

The method of procuring a project including the assembling of the project team.

Procurement route

The specific method of appointing a contractor.

Project information model (PIM)

The BIM model shared by the design team in a common data environment prior to and during construction.

Site appraisals

An appraisal used to determine the suitability of a site or sites at Stage 0.

Snagging list

A term used in the UK to define defects identified at Practical Completion. The snagging list may incorporate incomplete items where this has been agreed with the client.

Soft Landings

An initiative by BSRIA focused around the handover of a building and the subsequent processes that can improve the use of the building and lead to improvements on future projects.

Specification

The document used to define the materials and components to be used on a project, as well as the quality and workmanship standards required. Specifications can be:

descriptive
where a material or component is specified in a manner that allows the contractor to select a product. A reference product may be included within the specification

outline
a specification produced in the early stages of a project to assist with client sign-off and the preparation of Cost Information, including the construction cost estimate

performance
where a material or component is specified on the basis of design intent and performance criteria

prescriptive
where a material or component is specified in such a manner that no alternative may be used.

TotEx

Total project costs – this would comprise the CapEx and OpEx costs as well as all of the costs associated with the use of a building. For example, the costs of nurses and doctors in a hospital would be part of the TotEx cost.

Uniclass

An industry-standard classification system for construction products and information, published by the Construction Product Information Committee (CPIC)

RIBA Plan of Work 2013 glossary

A number of new themes and subject matters have been included in the RIBA Plan of Work 2013. The following presents a glossary of all of the capitalised terms that are used throughout the RIBA Plan of Work 2013. Defining certain terms has been necessary to clarify the intent of a term, to provide additional insight into the purpose of certain terms and to ensure consistency in the interpretation of the RIBA Plan of Work 2013.

'As-constructed' Information

Information produced at the end of a project to represent what has been constructed. This will comprise a mixture of 'as-built' information from specialist subcontractors and the 'final construction issue' from design team members. Clients may also wish to undertake 'as-built' surveys using new surveying technologies to bring a further degree of accuracy to this information.

Building Contract

The contract between the client and the contractor for the construction of the project. In some instances, the **Building Contract** may contain design duties for specialist subcontractors and/or design team members. On some projects, more than one Building Contract may be required; for example, one for shell and core works and another for furniture, fitting and equipment aspects.

Building Information Modelling (BIM)

BIM is widely used as the acronym for 'Building Information Modelling', which is commonly defined (using the Construction Project Information Committee (CPIC) definition) as: 'digital representation of physical and functional characteristics of a facility creating a shared knowledge resource for information about it and forming a reliable basis for decisions during

its life cycle, from earliest conception to demolition'.

Business Case

The **Business Case** for a project is the rationale behind the initiation of a new building project. It may consist solely of a reasoned argument. It may contain supporting information, financial appraisals or other background information. It should also highlight initial considerations for the **Project Outcomes**. In summary, it is a combination of objective and subjective considerations. The **Business Case** might be prepared in relation to, for example, appraising a number of sites or in relation to assessing a refurbishment against a new build option

Change Control Procedures

Procedures for controlling changes to the design and construction following the sign-off of the Stage 2 Concept Design and the **Final Project Brief**.

Common Standards

Publicly available standards frequently used to define project and design management processes in relation to the briefing, designing, constructing, maintaining, operating and use of a building.

Communication Strategy

The strategy that sets out when the project team will meet, how they will communicate effectively and the protocols for issuing information between the various parties, both informally and at Information Exchanges.

Construction Programme

The period in the **Project Programme** and the **Building Contract** for the construction of the project, commencing on the site mobilisation date and ending at **Practical Completion**.

Construction Strategy

A strategy that considers specific aspects of the design that may affect the buildability or logistics of constructing a project, or may affect health and safety aspects. The **Construction Strategy** comprises items such as cranage, site access and accommodation locations, reviews of the supply chain and sources of materials, and specific buildability items, such as the choice of frame (steel or concrete) or the installation of larger items of plant. On a smaller project, the strategy may be restricted to the location of site cabins and storage, and the ability to transport materials up an existing staircase.

Contractor's Proposals

Proposals presented by a contractor to the client in response to a tender that includes the **Employer's Requirements**. The **Contractor's Proposals** may match the **Employer's Requirements**, although certain aspects may be varied based on value engineered solutions and additional information may be submitted to clarify what is included in the tender. The **Contractor's Proposals** form an integral component of the **Building Contract** documentation.

Contractual Tree

A diagram that clarifies the contractual relationship between the client and the parties undertaking the roles required on a project.

Cost Information

All of the project costs, including the cost estimate and life cycle costs where required.

Design Programme

A programme setting out the strategic dates in relation to the design process. It is aligned with the **Project Programme** but is strategic in its nature, due to the iterative nature of the design process, particularly in the early stages.

Design Queries

Queries relating to the design arising from the site, typically managed using a contractor's in-house request for information (RFI) or technical query (TQ) process.

Design Responsibility Matrix

A matrix that sets out who is responsible for designing each aspect of the project and when. This document sets out the extent of any performance specified design. The **Design Responsibility Matrix** is created at a strategic level at Stage 1 and fine tuned in response to the Concept Design at the end of Stage 2 in order to ensure that there are no design responsibility ambiguities at Stages 3, 4 and 5.

Employer's Requirements

Proposals prepared by design team members. The level of detail will depend on the stage at which the tender is issued to the contractor. The **Employer's Requirements** may comprise a mixture of prescriptive elements and descriptive elements to allow the contractor a degree of flexibility in determining the **Contractor's Proposals**.

Feasibility Studies

Studies undertaken on a given site to test the feasibility of the **Initial Project Brief** on a specific site or in a specific context and to consider how site-wide issues will be addressed.

Feedback

Feedback from the project team, including the end users, following completion of a building.

Final Project Brief

The **Initial Project Brief** amended so that it is aligned with the Concept Design and any briefing decisions made during Stage 2. (Both the Concept Design and **Initial Project Brief** are Information Exchanges at the end of Stage 2.)

Handover Strategy

The strategy for handing over a building, including the requirements for phased handovers, commissioning, training of staff or other factors crucial to the successful occupation of a building. On some projects, the Building Services Research and Information Association (BSRIA) Soft Landings process is used as the basis for formulating the strategy and undertaking a **Post-occupancy Evaluation** (www.bsria.co.uk/services/design/soft-landings/).

Health and Safety Strategy

The strategy covering all aspects of health and safety on the project, outlining legislative requirements as well as other project initiatives, including the **Maintenance and Operational Strategy**.

Information Exchange

The formal issue of information for review

and sign-off by the client at key stages of the project. The project team may also have additional formal **Information Exchanges** as well as the many informal exchanges that occur during the iterative design process.

Initial Project Brief

The brief prepared following discussions with the client to ascertain the **Project Objectives**, the client's **Business Case** and, in certain instances, in response to site **Feasibility Studies**.

Maintenance and Operational Strategy

The strategy for the maintenance and operation of a building, including details of any specific plant required to replace components.

Post-occupancy Evaluation

Evaluation undertaken post occupancy to determine whether the **Project Outcomes**, both subjective and objective, set out in the **Final Project Brief** have been achieved.

Practical Completion

Practical Completion is a contractual term used in the **Building Contract** to signify the date on which a project is handed over to the client. The date triggers a number of contractual mechanisms.

Project Budget

The client's budget for the project, which may include the construction cost as well as the cost of certain items required post completion and during the project's operational use.

Project Execution Plan

The **Project Execution Plan** is produced in collaboration between the project lead and lead designer, with contributions from other designers and members of the project team. The **Project Execution Plan** sets out the processes and protocols to be used to develop the design. It is sometimes referred to as a project quality plan.

Project Information

Information, including models, documents, specifications, schedules and spreadsheets, issued between parties during each stage and in formal Information Exchanges at the end of each stage.

Project Objectives

The client's key objectives as set out in the **Initial Project Brief**. The document includes, where appropriate, the employer's **Business Case**, **Sustainability Aspirations** or other aspects that may influence the preparation of the brief and, in turn, the Concept Design stage. For example, **Feasibility Studies** may be required in order to test the **Initial Project Brief** against a given site, allowing certain high-level briefing issues to be considered before design work commences in earnest.

Project Outcomes

The desired outcomes for the project (for example, in the case of a hospital this might be a reduction in recovery times). The outcomes may include operational aspects and a mixture of subjective and objective criteria.

Project Performance

The performance of the project, determined using **Feedback**, including about the performance of the project team and the performance of the building against the desired **Project Outcomes**.

Project Programme

The overall period for the briefing, design, construction and post-completion activities of a project.

Project Roles Table

A table that sets out the roles required on a project as well as defining the stages during which those roles are required and the parties responsible for carrying out the roles.

Project Strategies

The strategies developed in parallel with the Concept Design to support the design and, in certain instances, to respond to the **Final Project Brief** as it is concluded. These strategies typically include:

- acoustic strategy
- fire engineering strategy
- **Maintenance and Operational Strategy**
- **Sustainability Strategy**
- building control strategy
- **Technology Strategy.**

These strategies are usually prepared in outline at Stage 2 and in detail at Stage 3, with the recommendations absorbed into the Stage 4 outputs and Information Exchanges.

The strategies are not typically used for construction purposes because they may contain recommendations or information that contradict the drawn information. The intention is that they should be transferred into the various models or drawn information.

Quality Objectives

The objectives that set out the quality aspects of a project. The objectives may comprise both subjective and objective aspects, although subjective aspects may be subject to a design quality indicator (DQI) benchmark review during the **Feedback** period.

Research and Development

Project-specific research and development responding to the **Initial Project Brief** or in response to the Concept Design as it is developed.

Risk Assessment

The **Risk Assessment** considers the various design and other risks on a project and how each risk will be managed and the party responsible for managing each risk.

Schedule of Services

A list of specific services and tasks to be undertaken by a party involved in the project which is incorporated into their professional services contract.

Site Information

Specific **Project Information** in the form of specialist surveys or reports relating to the project- or site-specific context.

Strategic Brief

The brief prepared to enable the Strategic Definition of the project. Strategic considerations might include considering different sites, whether to extend, refurbish or build new and the key **Project Outcomes** as well as initial considerations for the **Project Programme** and assembling the project team.

Sustainability Aspirations

The client's aspirations for sustainability, which may include additional objectives, measures or specific levels of performance in relation to international standards, as well as details of specific demands in relation to operational or facilities management issues.

The **Sustainability Strategy** will be prepared in response to the **Sustainability Aspirations** and will include specific additional items, such as an energy plan and ecology plan and the design life of the building, as appropriate.

Sustainability Strategy

The strategy for delivering the **Sustainability Aspirations**.

Technology Strategy

The strategy established at the outset of a project that sets out technologies, including Building Information Modelling (BIM) and any supporting processes, and the specific software packages that each member of the project team will use. Any interoperability issues can then be addressed before the design phases commence.

This strategy also considers how information is to be communicated (by email, file transfer protocol (FTP) site or using a managed third party common data environment) as well as the file formats in which information will provided. The **Project Execution Plan** records agreements made.

Work in Progress

Work in Progress is ongoing design work that is issued between designers to facilitate the iterative coordination of each designer's output. Work issued as **Work in Progress** is signed off by the internal design processes of each designer and is checked and coordinated by the lead designer.

Index